Behind the Curtain:
A Career in Equal Employment & Education Opportunity

Charles E. Duffy

dp
Drinian Press/

Behind the Curtain:
A Career in Equal Employment & Education Opportunity
Duffy, Charles Emmett

Events, locales, and conversations contained in this book are from the author's memory. In order to maintain the anonymity of the people involved, the author has, in some instances, changed the names of individuals and places or truncated conversations of several people into a single dialogue. Identifying characteristics and details such as physical properties, occupations and places of residence have sometimes been modified.

Drinian Press, LLC
P.O. Box 63
Huron, Ohio 44839

Visit our website at DrinianPress.com.

Cover design by Drinian Press LLC

Library of Congress Control Number: 2012936145

ISBN-10: 0-9833069-2-3
ISBN-13: 978-0-9833069-2-4

Printed in the United States of America

Contents

To Jackie

PROLOGUE

Federal employees and the civil service in general—the mindless, faceless bureaucrats—are often the brunt of jokes. During my career I saw the intersection of government and the private sector. I experienced nothing that conveyed the sense that one side or the other has cornered the market on good sense and intelligent practice.

Like the cases I encountered, the stories I tell are episodic. It was easy to get very "up" or very "down" over the outcome of any single case. I succumbed to this often, especially in my early years or on the bigger cases. The long-term truth is, however, that a career is made up of hundreds or thousands of cases, especially if one is in management for a long time. Almost always, no *one* case makes or breaks a career. The nationwide impact, that one person can have, is from constantly "banging away" at the overall issues. That impact can be increased if one is in a position to hire, train, and motivate people to, likewise, do good cases and keep "banging away." Finally, it must be realized that many of the gains will come from other sources or unintended consequences.

*****

My grandfather was born in 1882. He was too young to serve in the Spanish-American War and too old to be drafted into World War I. While I studied American History in college, I loved to hear his firsthand perspective on historical figures such as Woodrow Wilson or Harry Truman. He wasn't an out of touch old-timer, and he didn't rant; thus I loved getting his perspective. To put it another way, I always liked the stories the old-timers tell. If one puts enough stories together, one has a version of history.

My own mini-history is just a small part of the larger history of the American civil rights regulatory structure. It is not an evolutionary tale for which the ending has been written. The fact is that the most important and seemingly timeless truisms change all the time.

Historians and social scientists have the luxury of documenting change in increments of decades and centuries. We think, mostly, in terms of great leaps caused by inventions, plagues, wars. What I think most of us fail to see, however, is the incremental changes that add up quickly in one-work lifetime. This book is meant to explore one little niche of the recent American experience—mostly, I hope, through humor and irony.

I remember that when I was an undergrad and in graduate school in the late sixties, I learned two immutable *facts!* They were not presented as laws of nature, but rather as statements that had always, and would always, be true. The first was that the U.S. would always have a trade surplus. The second was that, while it was nice that women could vote, for purposes of studying voting behavior, it was irrelevant because women would always vote like their husbands, if married, or their fathers, if not. How many decades now have we had both a gender gap and a trade deficit?

The "LIFO" (Last in, first out) rule that applies rigidly in labor contracts also roughly applies in white-collar and professional jobs. Labor and unemployment cycles wax and wane every few years. As a result, workers at all educational levels will average better or worse employment records, promotions, and pay over a career simply on the basis of when, in the labor cycle, they graduate.

In my era, as it is today, if one graduated at the beginning of a boom time (and didn't go into a dying industry in a dying city), one probably built up enough seniority (or, in a white-collar job, experience) to withstand layoffs and, thus, have a smooth work life.

I left school when jobs were plentiful. My big "problem" was picking from among the available jobs. This was not a result of any great virtue or achievement on my part. It was just the time. Those who entered the job market several years earlier or several years later with similar records to mine did not usually fare as well as I, or if they did, they needed to expend more effort than I did.

It has been more than forty years since I started working for the federal government. Hopefully, these stories are useful public policy analysis; or the reader could just consider them the ranting of an out of touch old-timer.

Sometimes I wonder if there is any way to put my life with the feds in perspective. The big trends seem explainable, but some of the individual stories seem too over-the-top to be true. I've been told that fiction has to be believable, or the reader will be disenchanted. On the other hand, what does one do when the truth is strange?

Well, all that follows happened, and mostly as I tell it. I've changed many of the names and some places to protect the innocent. By the innocent, I mean me!

Anyone, who has burrowed deeply enough into the federal civil rights bureaucracy, has similar stories to tell. I found, however, that much of what I'm about to discuss is not spoken aloud, even on the inside. Most of us have heard how the federal EEO and Affirmative Action effort lives under the characterization of either "all good" or "all bad".

This is an insider's tale. I find that things that I have learned to take for granted—especially the history—are not commonly known or appreciated. Probably the old-timers in any field could say the same thing. There is an old adage that tells us that we don't want to see the sausage being made. It applies to both good sausage and bad sausage. My point is this: that Civil Rights enforcement is like sausage being made. The process wasn't always pretty to see. Still, the sausage came out tasting pretty good.

There is no "It was a dark and stormy night" way to start this story of the bureaucracy. I always felt I was a civil rights worker—and I was. But the context was the federal bureaucracy.

While I hope they will read it, this was not written to debate fine points in EEO law or to illuminate sub-regulations to practitioners, labor lawyers, or EEO professionals. For those people it is meant to amuse and, perhaps, allow a broader than normal look at Equal Employment issues. To those persons who aren't experts in EEO matters, it is meant to amuse and illustrate civil rights issues, mostly in employment, from the late 1960s on.

I have split this book into two parts. The first part is stories that are generally arranged chronologically. I hope that they'll be found humorous, wry, ironic, or whatever, depending on the story. Maybe these stories will even get a point or two across. That is for the reader to decide.

The second part contains a series of discussions and my personal opinions around the topic of civil rights in employment and education. In part, I just wanted to put my opinion "out there". In part, I wanted the reader of Part I to know that, yes; I know some of these stories raise serious issues. If the reader does not want to read anything but funny stories, skip Part II.

It wasn't my intention to spend over thirty years on civil rights issues for the federal government. I wasn't even sure, when I took the job at IRS, that I wanted to work for the federal government. I liked teaching, but felt I needed to finish my Ph.D. work if I was going to teach in higher education (beyond the one year I did). In the meantime, my family needed to eat.

Part I

Stories and Anecdotes

The IRS

The only part of my federal career not in civil rights was spent as a management intern at the IRS headquarters. The IRS' idea was to provide orientation through some general seminars. Added to that, there were six-week assignments in six different areas of management. After two years or so, one would settle into one area, having been promoted several times and fast-tracked. The trouble was that: the jobs were boring and only took a few hours a week each. At the time I told people that IRS treated us well, but gave us no important work until our hair fell out or turned grey. To compensate for how easy the work was I took two assignments at the same time without telling my supervisors. Not only that, but I still had time to read both Washington D.C. daily papers while on the job. Eventually, my hair, that didn't fall out, turned grey, but this didn't happen until decades after I left IRS.

*****

I was in my early twenties then; married, but not blind. The building started being flooded with twenty to twenty-two year old beauties. I asked around to find out what happened. It turned out that one of my fellow interns—a sec-

ond year, single guy, who was also in his early twenties—
had been put in charge of disadvantaged college student
summer hiring. I'm not sure what the disadvantage of being
pretty is, but I do know that plenty of Generals' and Senators' daughters were hired, and that he dated quite a few of
them.

The head of the intern program was a nice guy, but the
guy who hired the interns was a misogynist, as well as ra-
cially bigoted. He once took his staff to a porn flick as an
office "thank you" for a job well done. Times have changed,
I hope.

*****

Three of my assignments stick in my head.

The first assignment was helping to select the color of office furniture and room dividers that were to be used at taxpayer centers. The choice was either orange or blue, I forget
which one, but I was tasked with finding out which color
put taxpayers in the psychological frame of mind to pay
more taxes. The guy who sat at the desk next to mine was a
retired Colonel, double dipping, and he referred to anyone
against the Viet Nam War as *CommieHippiePeaceQueer* (said as
all one word).

Next, I was put on a team that was trying to dumb down
the 1040 to a fifth grade reading level. Instead of the word
Spouse, I suggested we substitute the words, *"husband or wife."*

"No," our lawyers said, "that's a legal term and must
stay."

"How 'bout parentheses after *spouse* surrounding the
words *husband or wife?*" I asked.

"Can't be done," they said.

Years later the impossible happened. The change was
made, but it was many years after I left the committee.

Finally, and there is no point to this story—I just like it.
Personal computers were just beginning to be used, and

were still rare in offices. Nonetheless I was tasked with finding the right PC and software for calculating depreciation on gravel piles caused by weather. Someone thought that a software application would be easier and more time efficient for determining losses than the current "system" (I use the term loosely). There were three agents nationwide who were employed to make such calculations. The system required that three persons (the pile owner, an expert neutral person, and the auditing agent) stand equidistant around the base of the pile. Each would estimate the loss, and then they'd average the estimated depreciation. For example, the presumption is that each one of the three guesses what percentage of the pile has been washed away by rain. Continuing in this example, the owner says 10%, the expert, 15%, and the agent, 20% so the average of 15% is used as the basis for depreciation.

The IRS thought this wasn't necessarily the best way to figure gravel pile depreciation; therefore, I was sent out to find a software program. I was given six weeks, full-time to find a suitable program.

Several years later, I happened to run into one of my former intern buddies in the basement cafeteria of a federal building. After catching up with the news about his divorce, his ex-wife and son moving back to California, I asked, "Dave, how's the gravel pile software working?"

His response: "Oh, they dropped it after a couple of years. They like the old way better!"

*****

After I'd been at IRS a few months, I received an invitation to a White House reception. The reception was being held during the day, and I was to be paid to attend. I was pleased by the invitation, but didn't understand. Why me? I was told not to worry, but to just go to the assigned gate at the assigned time. Before I actually got to the gate, what was going on began to be clear to me. There were a lot of buses with military logos from all the bases around Washington parked nearby.

What was going on was a greeting for the King of Jordan. They needed a crowd, but there were few Jordanians in Washington and few Americans who cared enough to come. So I became part of the crowd that supplemented the military families who got a free ride into Washington for some sightseeing and shopping after the "reception". This was something done in Washington all the time.

We never got inside the White House, but I was put in the first row and had a great view. Only two things stood out in my memory of that day. First, close up President Nixon looked pretty normal and not at all like his caricatures or image on black and white TV. Second, King Hussein was downright eloquent.

*****

During part of my tenure, my office was on the first floor in the IRS headquarters, which is located at 11th and Constitution. During that time, the Viet Nam protests came to D.C. Our offices were next to the Department of Justice. The building also housed the FBI headquarters, which was soon to be moved to a location of its own.

During one of the daytime protests, Attorney General Mitchell came out on the balcony and goaded the crowd. When they howled and surged, the police dutifully gassed them. Unfortunately, the prevailing breeze was such that the tear gas came right through the first floor at the IRS. While I took part in the peaceful nighttime march, I got gassed during the day while sitting at a desk. I guess I was a true *CommieHippiePeaceQueer* and, apparently, deserved it. However, the gas didn't discriminate, and the retired colonel, who sat next to me, also ended up with burning, tearing eyes.

After only five months at the IRS, I decided it was time to go. The new Equal Employment Opportunity Commission was expanding and looking for more staff. I was offered jobs in Washington, but, after IRS, I wanted to get out there into the real world of investigations where, as my second EEOC supervisor told me, you get to "slay the discrimination dragon". Yes, we really talked this way; however, when it was late in the day, we also talked of how the "dragon" had been there for hundreds of years and how it would be there tomorrow.

EEOC investigations might be more fun than working out depreciation on gravel piles, and, I thought, might even be socially useful.

At IRS I regularly rode the bus into work from Alexandria. The Assistant Commissioner for Administration often rode the same bus. He was a real bigwig, but it was a rarity to see anyone of his stature on a bus. Because of his bus riding, he was really approachable, and I got to know him. During a commute in my last week, he said he had heard that I was leaving IRS and asked me why. Dropping my big whistleblower bombshell, I said, "No one works over half time in that building."

His answer: "So?"

The EEOC

"Training" and First Cases at EEOC

Most of my career was spent reviewing personnel practices and other standards of American industry. What I discovered was that the looniness of government was matched in private enterprise. The human resource activities at companies that were complained about in 1969-1971 were considered plenty strange, too—at least by today's standards. One of my elders liked to jokingly start speeches to business groups by saying, "You are too male and too pale." At that time most HR types, which were then called "personnel managers", were middle-aged white males. By the time I, a middle-aged white male, retired, most HR types were female, minority, young, or some combination of the three.

Back then, EEOC's cases garnered a guilty finding rate of over 60%. Now, I think it's less than 5%.

In retrospect, my first three cases seem wild. On my first case, I was told to observe and be quiet while my supervisor/trainer interviewed the personnel manager. At issue in this case was whether the company hired qualified women applicants to all jobs. The manager assured us that he did indeed hire woman for all jobs, and then more discussion followed. My trainer could not see out the window that I was sitting beside, but I did. Just a few feet from the window hung the company's HELP WANTED sign. It read:

> VACANCIES
> Men:
> Machine Repair
> Maintenance Men
> Loaders
> Women:
> Typists
> Light Assembly

My instructions had been to only observe; I felt like the kid in class who knows the answer, jumps up and down waving, but isn't called on by the teacher. This was not a "sign"—an allegory or parable; it was a statement, a literal sign, in black and white that this company did not hire women for some jobs, and it hung before my eyes.

In retrospect, something else happened on that investigation that illustrated the times. Here was Rick, a great trainer, and a "slam dunk" sex discrimination case. Before the interview the personnel manager had the secretary bring coffee. I heard her say, "Mr. Johnson (Rick), would you like anything in your coffee?"

His response: "No honey, just swirl your finger in it and that'll sweeten it enough."

Everyone chuckled politely, and no one said they thought it was an inappropriate remark (for the times). Whether or not the secretary mentally gagged, I never knew.

At least once, Rick, himself, was on the receiving end of insensitivity. Someone at EEOC apparently disparaged his Lebanese ancestry because I heard him respond: "Listen, my people had an alphabet, math, a navy, and a civil society for a thousand years while your people were still painting themselves blue and worshipping trees!"

While still in his thirties, Rick went on to have a heart attack on the job. My office partner was sent to the hospital by the District Director to give him an armful of case files. "What?!" said the Director when everyone looked aghast. "He's just sitting around anyway."

Early EEOC was not a place full of lazy government employees. Rick was just one of three guys to have heart attacks when I was working at the Cleveland office of EEOC. Another guy, who had a heart attack, came back to work very peeved that no one from the office had called or sent a "Get Well" card during the whole six weeks he was out. Frankly, the reason no one called was that no one in management bothered telling anyone else where Art was. Our business may have been funny, but it was *serious* funny business.

*****

On my second training case, a lady brought in a letter signed by the company president saying that, because she had filed a human rights complaint against the company, she would not get any overtime while the complaint was in effect. We couldn't believe the letter was real so we went out to ask the president for his reaction.

He said, and I remember this more than forty years later, "I hired Negroes before it was fashionable." The man had been charged with denying overtime because a complaint had been filed, and his defense was that he hired African Americans "before it was fashionable."

Handing the president a copy of the letter, Rick, my trainer, asked him, "Yes, but what about the letter?"

The man rose, put his right hand on his chest and looking at the ceiling cried, "Is there no protection for the righteous? This case is a stench in the nostrils of the public." (I am *not* making this up!)

He followed with, "I want you out of my office and off my property."

"You can't do that. They have the right to investigate the complaint. It is the law now," said the personnel manager.

After a few minutes of muttering and grumbling, the president said, "I wanted to fire her for having the nerve to file a charge but, since my lawyer told me I couldn't, I just denied her overtime to get even."

*****

Since I had been out in the field for two cases, it was decided that for my third case, I would be allowed to observe my first negotiation. The case involved a casket company where two married employees—not married to each other and, I suppose these days I need to point out, of different genders—were observed having sex in a casket in the plant. The woman was immediately fired for such unladylike behavior but, the company's attitude was that of "boys will be boys," so the man was not fired, only warned.

The woman immediately filed a charge of wrongful termination due to gender. (I have no idea what she told her husband, or if that mattered.) We found for her, and negotiation ensued. The attorney for the company had clearly told the company that they were dead. I know this; the attorney opened the meeting by saying, "I know we are dead on the firing issue."

The recent Scottish immigrant HR director, clearly confused at his company being found guilty, stated in a heavy burr that he had just done what he thought was right, but he'd been told that they were guilty. As far as I know, he never saw that the issue was choosing to fire one employee because of gender while keeping the other despite the fact that both of their actions were the same.

As bizarre to me as the actions of the company was the behavior of our Conciliator.

After the company lawyer conceded guilt, our Conciliator responded: "Discrimination is invidious."

The HR Director looked even more confused than he had been about the guilty finding, but he continued and offered to hire the woman back.

"Discrimination is invidious," intoned the Conciliator.

The company offered back pay.

"Discrimination is invidious, "came the reply.

The company offered interest and benefits.

Again, "Discrimination is invidious."

I think the company settled, but I'm not sure because I left the room after the fifth or sixth hearing of "discrimination is invidious". I went and got a dictionary and looked up the word, *invidious*, and agree to this day that discrimination is, indeed, invidious.

*****

Until this time I was tagging along with an experienced investigator or watching a conciliator. Now after reading what little case law was available, I was deemed ready for my first solo case. For the last thirty years, investigators were trained for years before being unleashed on the public; however, I was given just two months' training before being sent out alone. Glad for the apparent confidence management had in me, I was, nonetheless, nervous to be on my own.

It was Christmas Eve 1969, but I was too new to have any vacation built up, so out I went into a snowstorm to my appointment at the complainant's house in Elyria, Ohio. Her complaint was that she had been fired for being pregnant.

I was invited into the small living room where the woman, her girlfriend, her mother-in-law, her (brand new) baby, her six-year-old twins, her friend's eight-year-old child, and an aunt and uncle were gathered. All of the adults, complainant included, were tipsy on blackberry wine, which they kept offering me.

I suggested to the new mother that we go into the kitchen for our interview. She brought her infant and friend, who was also a co-worker, and then proceeded to breast-feed the baby. Despite the bedlam in the house, all went well until I asked her whether the company medical plan had covered the birth of her child. She didn't know the answer, and I continued my interview.

Her friend proceeded to go to the phone, called the Human Resources Department, and asked if, when the company fires pregnant women, it also cuts off medical coverage. The HR manager said, "Yes."

"Aha!" said the tipsy friend, "there's an FBI man here and he is going to get you." So saying, she thrust the phone in my face and said, "Tell 'em." I declined and became just another government fink in their eyes. Later, I found in favor of the woman with the baby.

*****

In the Field

After my training and first solo case, things did not settle down. Often I was the first EEOC investigator to visit a site and, even if I were not the first, I was often first to be raising the type of issue my complainant raised.

Once, I was going out of town to do a "Big Three" auto case. While this auto company had a policy of not lying to investigators, they also had a policy of not answering any question not posed exactly the right way (which meant in their jargon). I was staying and eating at the local Holiday Inn. When I went out to eat, it became clear that the booth behind me held the Detroit rep and the local rep, and that they were discussing and prepping for the case. I asked the waiter for a pen, listened in, and wrote notes all over the disposable paper placemats. As I left the restaurant, during their dessert, I said, "See you tomorrow." At this, they looked confused. However, the next day, when I walked in, they looked crestfallen. I got all the information I needed for the case. On the other hand, I don't remember a thing about the case and whether or not the company was guilty.

*****

One of my first cases in Michigan was also my first big Hispanic class case. There was a saying in that part of the state that went: if you ain't Dutch, you ain't much.

I took rookie, Pedro Alvarez Del Azullo, to translate. He was a Mexican American from Texas. The class members were mostly recent, legal immigrants, originally from South and Central America.

They didn't like Mexicans. Pedro didn't like Central and South Americans much, either. I was so ignorant that I thought all Spanish-speaking people got along. Pedro and I spent the day before we went on-site (to the company) interviewing the class members one by one in my motel room, located on the outskirts of the small town.

It's not as if we had a suite in which to interview. Government *per diem* did not allow for that so we just used my "cheapie" room with the bed that sagged, and the room that still smelled moldy and humid despite the wall heater running because of the snow outside. We started around 8:00 am and finished well after dark.

The gist of the complaints was that Hispanics were treated worse (on the job) than the Anglos. For example, Anglos got free lab coats, while the Hispanics didn't. There was also an all-female line of pickle packers who each put two pickles in; however, where the person stood in that line made a difference. Anglo women got to put the first pickles in, and Hispanics had to push down to get the last ones in the jar. The employee pushing in the last pickles sometimes cut her hands on the ragged glass, and, given that the employees were working in brine, this could be both nasty and disabling.

Worse, the foreman called all Hispanics, regardless of gender, "Pancho" and felt free to grab them by the arm to move them around. The men, especially the macho men, really didn't like this guy grabbing their wives. One complainant (Jesus) jumped over the assembly line to get at the foreman after he had grabbed his wife. Others intervened; Jesus never got to the foreman, but he was still fired for the attempt.

When we interviewed Jesus about his wife being grabbed, I asked Pedro to ask Jesus what he thought of Fred Estoberger, the foreman. At this, Jesus pulled out a knife, jumped on the bed, and began waving the knife and yelling. While I didn't understand much Spanish then, I caught a fragment which was "Fred Estoberger—morte!" A few minutes later, when the complainant settled down, I asked Pedro what had been said.

Pedro replied, "He doesn't like his boss." Thank God I had a translator. By the way, the company was guilty.

*****

There was a foundry in Cleveland in which the following conversation occurred.

Me (to the personnel manager): "Do you have any problems hiring blacks and Hispanics?"

"No," he said, "but with blacks and Hispanics at the bottom of the economic scale, you'd think they be more available than at the 40% rate I'm hiring them at. Everyone knows blacks love heat and Puerto Ricans are big and burly."

"You know," I said, "if you insist on stereotyping, please get the stereotypes right. You just reversed them."

I couldn't fault his hiring practices even though the turnover rate ran 100% in the blue-collar workforce.

*****

There was another company near the foundry where, upon being presented with a charge of individual race and sex discrimination in hiring, officials insisted they were not bigots.

"Why," said the manager, "if that Negro lady had been a man, we'd have hired her right away." He then went on to

list a whole group of jobs for which they didn't consider any
woman.

*****

Sometimes the company was so bigoted (in its hiring
procedures) that we couldn't believe it. I was given a case
that involved a trucking company that had earlier been
found guilty of discrimination against minority applicants.
As remedy, they went back and hired ten "victims"—well-
qualified minority applicants they had discriminated
against—for their next ten openings.

Months later, an African American complainant came in
to EEOC and said that while he was the best qualified, he
had been refused a job at the company because they said,
"We already have enough (minorities)."

Upon calling the company, we were told that, "Yes, the
guy is right. We hired those ten, and then went back to
'normal' hiring. What did you expect us to do? Keep hiring
minorities when we had just hired ten?"

This company did not just say that we don't want this
person as our eleventh hire. What they said was that after
the ten minorities, who had earlier been refused jobs because of their race and in spite of being best-qualified, were
hired, they weren't even going to look at the qualifications
of minority applicants that followed for any openings in the
foreseeable future. As a bonus, the personnel director continued by "explaining" that if the company started hiring
more minorities, we might get known on the East Side
(Cleveland code, even then, for the minority community) as
a place that hires blacks.

Some cases tended to generate "reasonable cause" (to believe the law was violated) findings, but still take only a few
hours. This was one of them.

*****

Occasionally, I ran into nutty complainants instead of just nutty companies. The agencies had to accept every complaint and investigate it from beginning to end, no matter what (the charge was). Usually the reason given for not allowing us to turn down complaints that were nutty on their face value was: "You aren't a psychiatrist." The regulations, we were told, said we receive complaints, not just *some* complaints. One of the agencies for which I later worked (HEW) finally allowed us to drop "frivolous" complaints. We wrote the HEW lawyers asking what "frivolous" meant in practice and sent them five examples. In return, we got back an eight-page memo ignoring the examples and essentially defining "frivolous" as "frivolous".

Sometimes everyone involved in a case seemed goofy. Early on, I received a notarized charge from a man who said he was fired for being late to work a few times while whites were not fired for the same offense. I could never find the man to interview him, but, because the charge was "perfected", which meant notarized, I had to investigate.

The case to be investigated was at a large UAW plant. In those days the auto companies were hiring, but this plant, in particular, hated to cooperate with us.

I went on-site and presented the charge. Company officials said the man was a 'three-day no-report" probationary employee. Anybody who missed three days or was late three times in his or her ninety-day probationary period was fired. They treated me correctly, if not civilly. I was able to find that for the two years up to and a few months after my complainant was hired, all persons of any race who were "three-day no-report" were fired—no exceptions.

I said I'd not been able to find the man, but they said, "Not our problem."

Then I proceeded to walk across the street to the union hall where I was to meet with the Business Agent. The allegation also was that the union failed to represent the complainant because he was black. Usually, only southern and construction unions were wild and nasty, but these were northern Ohio autoworkers so I didn't expect any trouble. I sat down across from the Business Agent, a white guy, and we began to talk. A minute later a large black man charged through the door behind me and addressed the Business Agent: "You honky bastard!"

The Business Agent responded in kind yelling, "You stupid nigger!"

The black man pulled a knife, and flew by me at the Business Agent, who pulled a Billy club from the desk. They grappled for a minute but, luckily for my heart, it looked fake from the start because there was neither blood nor a cracked skull.

Then they started to laugh. The black man introduced himself as the union president and put the knife down. "You really don't know, do you?" he said.

I said, "Know what?"

"You haven't been able to find him (the complainant), have you?"

Defensively, I said, "No, but the charge is perfected so it's valid and I need to know why you didn't represent him." Unions had few representative duties for probationary workers, but they had some. Equal treatment, also, was required.

"We didn't need him working here. Those idiots across the street were just jerking you around, but here is all you need," said the Business Agent, pulling a file of newspaper clippings from his desk.

"You'll find whatever you need there and can copy what you want down the hall." At that, he and the Chapter President left the room laughing. I sat down to read the *Plain Dealer* clippings.

Through reading these clippings, I deduced the following:

One day my missing complainant got a ride to work from his wife, who crashed the car during the drive in to work. She had to go to the hospital so he missed Day One.

A couple days later, he went to pick her up from the hospital, but got so irate at her for causing him to miss work that he, subsequently, broke her wrist and damaged her skull. Although his wife wouldn't press charges, the complainant still missed Day Two.

A few days later, his wife was, again, to be released from the hospital. He went to pick her up and was still mad. This time, he poured lighter fluid on her bandages and lit them. However, the hospital was able to file charges so the complainant missed Day Three. Had he not been fired, our "Husband of the Year" candidate would also have missed every other day since he was scheduled to be in prison for a long time.

*****

Another time a "perfected" case came back and bit me occurred during one of my first conciliations. At the time investigators, decision writers, and conciliators (negotiators) were split into different units. No one had ever talked to the victim, but her charge had been notarized. I tried to find her before the negotiation, but was unsuccessful in my attempt. Although she had filed the complaint, the finding itself was a "class" finding, meaning that we found for all women.

Two lawyers, representing the company, flew in from Michigan. I told them how much money we wanted, and of the great troubles that awaited their client if they did not agree to pay.

The lead attorney asked, "Have you spoken to the complainant lately?"

Luckily, for once, I wasn't a smart ass. I told them simply, "No."

Smirking, they informed me that the complainant had died intestate—meaning without heirs.

In EEOC's early days complainants didn't have the independent go-to-court rights they've now had for decades. When they called our bluff, it meant that our only recourse was to get the Commission members to vote to send the case to the Attorney General for enforcement in federal court. President Nixon's Attorney General, at the time, was John Mitchell, and he was no friend of EEOC or its cases; therefore, Federal Court referral wasn't going to happen.

*****

Dealing with Company Counsel provided a lot of interesting moments. We were always fighting but, since they were just doing their jobs, I didn't really hold it against them. I was more likely to object to our own lawyers not being vigorous enough. Admittedly, my first several years in the field were spent fuming at these "evil beings" (company lawyers) who had the audacity to oppose me. I don't know if I matured, or just got tired.

On the phone one attorney opened his defense of his client thundering, "Lies, damn lies, and statistics!" Then more calmly, he said, "Thanks; this case will put one of my kids through college."

I had first encountered this lawyer previously. My first contact was via phone after we'd found against another client. He was representing a company that refused to hire a woman for second shift clerical duties because she'd have to leave (downtown) work after dark. The company's defense was that: "Everyone knows it isn't safe for women to be out after dark."

He told me that the finding was a clear miscarriage of justice because the job was a BFOQ—that you needed to be male to do the job. BFOQ stands for Bona Fide Occupational Qualification and means that gender is a job requirement. We used to joke that BFOQ only applied to wet nurses and sperm bank donors. I know of no case where this defense worked, much less this one.

I said, "You've got to be kidding."

He said, "Well, I tried. How much will this cost?"

It turned out that it cost the company very little because the complainant got a job very quickly after she had been turned down (by this company). It paid more than the one she was denied, and she liked it a lot better.

*****

Another fun case concerned a guy who was fired for getting too many company parking violations.

The company was the largest employer (25,000 employees) in a medium-sized city so parking was at a premium. The company had only been hiring minorities in large numbers in recent years, but parking spaces were allotted by seniority. Maybe you can see where I'm going with this. Only whites with at least fifteen years' seniority could park anywhere near, and by near I mean within a quarter mile of, the plant. The man had filed a charge that would be a no-brainer by 1985, but this occurred in 1970. He said the effect of the seniority rule for parking, given the fact that minorities had lesser seniority because of company inaction, made minorities lesser-treated in conditions of work (that is, the average minority employee couldn't park as close to the plant as the average white employee).

The company issued a warning and a ticket to anyone parking in someone else's spot. After the sixth ticket, the person was to be fired. Apprehension of violators was spotty and only one duty (of many) for the guards. The guards knew that minorities had lower seniority and that close-in parking was for high seniority folks. The policy was such that a guard didn't have to be a bigot to notice a black face getting out of the driver's side of a car at a close-in space where only white faces should be. Thus, not only was the policy wrong, but the enforcement was unintentionally biased, also.

The complainant kept parking close-in as a protest against the policy. The guards kept noticing. Eventually the complainant got fired and filed his charge.

For this case, I needed to not only understand the policy, but to check the equality of enforcement. This didn't discount the fact that a minority was more likely to be caught just because of skin color. I found that every minority was fired if he or she got a seventh ticket, as were some whites. However, some twenty-five whites had seven or more warnings and were still employed.

With straight faces, company representatives explained each and every of the twenty-five whites as a "special exception". Some of my favorites were the following:

The lady who was "not in her right mind" when she got three of the tickets;

The guy who also drove his daughter to work (one car, one driver although she had low seniority) so they were each entitled to six warnings before either was fired.

The group who worked "in another building" so the warnings didn't count although the policy didn't exempt the other building. Why ticket people exempted from ticketing?

It was cases like these where you wanted to say, "Listen to yourselves. Aren't you embarrassed?" Actually, I did say that once and the lawyer called my boss and said I was a Nazi. That's the old lawyers' trick: when you can't pound the facts or the law, pound the table.

*****

We had a lot of employees who were formerly part of Roman Catholic religious orders. This wasn't surprising given the exodus of many priests and nuns in the late '60s and early '70s. Social welfare-type/work was both their inclination and training. Almost all were good folks, but some were real characters.

My favorite was Antonio. He was an Italian National who went to a Spanish seminary. He told me he never fit in there because he wasn't Spanish. When he was ordained, he was sent from Spain to Texas because his order with its Spanish priests serviced the Hispanics of the Southwestern United States. After a while he thought that maybe he should rethink being a priest. He became a Green Beret Chaplain so, as he told me, he could review his options. He was soon sent to Viet Nam. While he was in Viet Nam, he met a Philippine Seventh Day Adventist nurse, left the priesthood, and got married.

One day, on the Saigon streets, he was offered a baby in exchange for one dollar. He declined, but then asked the "merchant" what he was going to do with the baby. The man said, "I guess I'll kill it." That's how Antonio got his son Donny.

Antonio told me his investigative technique was that he could tell by looking at a person whether he or she was lying. Since Antonio thought everyone was honest, he believed the last person with whom he spoke. *Evidence* was never a factor in his cases. Luckily for me, we were always co-workers and I was never his boss.

*****

The ultimate throwback was Ted Cielo. He was hired at EEOC when we only did sex, race, national origin, and religion cases. Ninety-five percent of the cases were race and sex cases. When he got his first sex case assigned, he said, "I don't go that shit." We asked him what that meant in English and he repeated, "I don't go that shit." Basically, he wouldn't do a gender case of any type and just let them sit. This was one of *our* employees.

*****

The Influence of a District Director

When a finding is sent out, it really matters to the employer, the school, the employees, or the students affected. The finding is a legal document, even if it is not a judge's ruling. It can be the basis of an appeal or the beginning reasoning behind a multimillion dollar negotiation.

In my early days working at the EEOC, my office partner was Mona; the director was Chas. Chas rejected two of Mona's cases as defamatory to the company when all she was doing was quoting their defense. Once she quoted someone as saying that the charge was: "bullshit." Chas rejected that. So Mona took the quotes out and then wrote: Fecal matter of the male bovine. Chas got the idea and let the quote stay.

In another case, the manager said that he fired two cooks because, he said, "they were hookers."

"Too inflammatory," said Chas.

"How is quoting a defense inflammatory?" Mona asked, to no avail.

With help Mona found 139 synonyms for the word *prostitute*, typed them up, and gave them to Chas, suggesting that he pick one. Several of us had lots of fun coming up with all those words and phrases. Not one of us had known all of them. Chas again relented and sent the finding out with the word *hooker* in quotes.

You might wonder how Mona had time to sit around looking for synonyms. In those days we were still working out the quality/quantity issue on cases. The production rate per investigator ran from four cases a month to one case a quarter. Mona was the one-case-per-quarter person, but credit had to be given to her. Her cases were so complete that we used to say that they could be delivered straight to the U.S. Supreme Court and everything else skipped in between.

The one-case-per-quarter estimate probably understated her output, but I know of several processions we had when Mona turned in a case for review. Word would spread in the hallway where our teams' offices were that Mona was about to turn in a (rare) case. Someone would decorate a file cover with pictures or phrases appropriate to the season to underscore the idea that this was a once-in-a-season event. I remember one file, in particular, that had pumpkins and ghosts on the cover. When Mona came out of her office to walk down the hall to turn the case into her supervisor, those on the rest of her team would line up like monks in a procession leading or following her down the hall chanting nonsense like: "Sancta autumncasefilum, Ora Pro Nobis."

Mona would continue down the hall, muttering, "Cut it out you guys. I turn in lots of cases. Stop it. Stop it!"

(Hang in with me, here; I'm not really changing topics.)

My next assignment was a case in which a Hungarian refugee, who was a foreman, had his jacket was ripped when he was thrown to the ground by his supervisor, the general foreman. The general foreman said, "You God-damned DP! Why don't you go back to Hungary where you came from?"

The foreman, an old-world gentleman, wanted only an apology and his coat repaired. He was told by the company's upper management that he couldn't file a complaint against a member of management. When he did, he was fired.

Everyone (on both sides) agreed that this is what had happened. I wrote the case up, finding national origin discrimination and retaliation, and I even quoted the general foreman. Once again the case was rejected as defamatory even though I argued, to no avail, that I was quoting the man.

Knowing what Mona had done in her cases with *hooker* and *B.S.,* I wrote instead that the general foreman had rent the foreman's garment while throwing him on the floor, then casting aspersions on his national origin, assigning him to perdition, invoking the Deity in the process.

I heard nothing about the case for a week, but then I received a phone call from the company's attorney who said, "What the heck is this?"

"What the heck is what?" I asked.

"This rending of garments and perdition crap."

Oops; Chas had failed to read my correction and issued the finding as I had rewritten it. I couldn't settle the case, and it went to court. I'll bet someone at court had a laugh over the finding.

*****

Many complainants don't understand the fact that although the Director issues the finding, it is the investigator who usually writes it up. This fact may have saved my life once when I was an investigator.

I was assigned a complaint from a man who said he was being harassed because of his race. The man had served twenty years for a murder committed while he was employed at the company. He was rehired when he was released. Rehiring a recently released murderer didn't strike me as great evidence of racial animus. Nonetheless the complainant, an African American, claimed that the Polish American women employees were all hitting on him. He further claimed that the foremen were spying on him.

It turned out that the women in the plant weren't chasing the man, but the foremen were watching to see if his charges regarding the women could be proven or not.

I wrote the case up, and Chas issued a *no cause* (not guilty) finding.

The next week, I was walking by our waiting area and saw my complainant calmly sitting there. I said, "Hi, Mr. *Jones.* How come you're here?"

He said, "Oh, Mr. Duffy. You are a nice man, but that Mr. *Charles*, he is a bad man. He wrote that finding; I have to kill him. Look." At this, he pulled up one pant leg and revealed a large bladed knife tucked down in his white sock.

I was a little stunned at this, and said something to the effect of: "Hold on. I'll see if Chas is here." Then I stepped through the doorway to Chas' secretary's desk and, out of the man's hearing, and asked her if Chas was in. She said he was. I then told her to tell him to go out the back way; that an angry complainant was here to kill him, no joke; and to call the police.

Then I went back through the waiting room and told the man that Chas would be a few minutes. His reaction to this was as if I had said, "The doctor is running late and will see you in ten minutes."

His response: "Okay."

In the meantime, I waited near the elevator for the two uniformed police officers. They arrived in a few minutes, but were skeptical. Nonetheless, one approached the man from the front entrance, the other from the back entrance and then calmly asked the man what he was doing there. The complainant told them the same thing he had told me. When he also lifted the leg of his pants to show the knife, after the briefest pause to glance, surprised, at each other, they jumped on him.

Chas never said a word to me about the incident, but, as a measure of EEOC's great internal labor relations, at least a couple employees muttered, I think in jest, something along the lines of "You shoulda let the guy kill him."

✳✳✳✳✳

It wasn't just that the Director suffered from the antipathy most employees feel towards their supervisors; we had more justification than most. For example, this EEOC District Director had a couch upon which no one could sit.

At the time we were taking in 200 charges a month so his boss asked for a plan to reduce the backlog. Chas' plan: to do 50 cases a month (thus creating a bigger backlog).

Perhaps, that should have been a clue about what was to come. Our building was, above the second floor, horseshoe-shaped. (It has subsequently been torn down and replaced by a Marriott and Key Corp. headquarters, but I digress.) Chas could look out across the horseshoe into the two-person investigators' offices. We received a couple intercom buzzes asking why Mona and I were talking, rather than working. Having assured him we *were* discussing investigations, I started dropping the old wooden-slatted Venetian blinds whenever we were talking cases. This prompted a memo that said blinds were to be up at all times so that Chas' view of his people wouldn't be blocked.

Chas also had the *"clean desk"* policy. At the end of every day, investigators were to put away all work and then take it out the following day. Chas felt this not only looked better (to whom, I always wondered), but that it also forced the investigator to be organized about what they took out to work on. Further, to prevent his people from just sweeping the desk clean into a drawer at the end of the day, he required all desks to remain unlocked so that he could inspect the contents to make sure things had been put away in an orderly manner.

I felt that these policies were Chas' problem, not mine and since they were in effect when I started, I just went along with them. Other investigators, no doubt those who were naturally disorganized, seethed at this policy. Nonetheless, when a private office across the hall from the horseshoe opened up, I jumped at the chance to move.

Later, Chas promoted me. I asked him why. Frankly, I was wondering if it was my super high case production, my great quality cases, or both that he had noticed. He told me that he promoted me because whenever he saw me in the halls, I was walking fast. Since I wanted the higher pay, I didn't remind him that I may have walked the fastest because I was the second youngest employee in the office.

I knew of no one who could kid Chas. My two attempts at humor fell flat although I will admit that one was a bit mean-spirited. When he originally interviewed me for the job, I made a remark that I didn't care if a person was black, white, male, female, or a Swedish dentist. He jumped at the last category and said, "What do you have against Swedes?" At that point, I had to explain I was being ridiculous.

Near the end of my time working for EEOC, I was the first union steward and we were having a bargaining meeting. For one thing, Chas didn't believe that there should be a union. Further, he felt that if there were to be a union, the steward should come in to meetings to be lectured about how things were to be. I didn't agree.

By the way, Chas happened to be black and was part of the Cleveland black aristocracy. He told me, notwithstanding his background, that he knew what it was like to be discriminated against. I expected to hear of lynching, house burnings, slurs, police harassment, or job denials in either his or his family's past because almost all of Cleveland's black community in the '60s had such legitimate family stories.

However, Chas told me that when he was at the private all-male college he attended in the 1930s, he was a cheerleader for the (what-I-assumed-was-the-all-or-nearly-all-white) basketball team. He told me that when the team and cheerleaders went to Cincinnati in the late 1930s that "they wouldn't let me sleep with the team."

I thought to myself: *This was the biggest negative that ever happened to him? He went to a private college.* Cheerleaders "sleeping" with the basketball team usually meant something entirely different. I told him, "They probably saved you from a life of moral degradation." He wasn't happy with me, and we made little progress.

*****

In those days Regional Counsel reported for legal guidance to Washington, and had a sort of tenant-landlord relationship with the District Director. Chas brought the Regional Counsel up on charges of destroying government property. The two men both flew to D.C. for a hearing in which Chas (the boss) claimed the counsel had failed to cover his typewriter at night before going home "on more than one occasion" as well as had been observed putting his feet up on his desk.

When it was his turn to reply, the Regional Counsel asked if the board had heard the charges. When he was assured they had, he said, "Good; that's my defense." The counsel was cleared.

*****

An old in-house EEOC story could be considered funny or not depending on the position one held…that is, whether you were the investigator, the supervisor, or the District Director. A case in point was the simple charge I had from a lady who said she was denied the right even to put in an application at a company because the company wouldn't hire women anyway. Early on, these charges were not uncommon, but they certainly presented a problem. How could the complainant even prove she'd been to the company? All the company had to do when presented the charge was say: "Jane Doe? Never heard of her."

I decided that since this was a complaint of gender discrimination, the company, if guilty, was probably being paternalistic and not antagonistic to the applicant. Both would violate the law, but my investigation would be different if they were just being paternalistic. I also felt that the company would probably not lie about the lady being there if they felt no threat. So, posing as a state unemployment bureau employee, I called to verify that the complainant had been there and was, thus, still eligible for continued unemployment benefits. The company confirmed she'd been there, and we went on to find the company guilty.

Chas hit the roof. We had based a guilty finding on a federal employee lying about being a state employee doing another job. At the time I thought his anger was a small price to pay for getting the evidence I needed. When I became a Regional and District Director, the thought that one of my investigators would pull such a stupid, shortsighted stunt made my frustration level rise even higher than it normally did. The old saying, that where you stand depends on where you sit, really applies.

A Stupid Move

While this story happened more than thirty-five years ago, I was too embarrassed to tell anyone for at least fifteen years. To put this in the proper perspective, you have to realize that in 1970 and '71 equal employment enforcement was still in its infancy. Many people didn't like what we were doing. Because of this, I was called "nigger lover" and then asked: "What are you working for *them* for?" (The *them* wasn't the government.) I was told more than once that this investigative work might seem like fun for a couple years, but, if I stayed too long, I would never get out and have a *real* career.

This continued this way for more than a decade, and I remember being at a party in which I was informed that it was okay to have women salespersons, but if the company expected to sell to a corporation, you'd need to deal at the Vice-Presidential level. My informant continued that it was absurd to think that a Vice-President would deal with a lady. Today, the company, that my misogynist storyteller represented, counts at least one woman among its ex-CEOs.

This is all to say that things have come a long way since I had a personnel director in Cleveland pull back his fist to hit me because I just relayed the news that I was finding against his company. At this point, I told him he'd go to prison if he hit me, and at this, he backed off.

There were instances where companies had us followed. They wanted to know to whom we talked and to see if there was any dirt they could get on us in order to discourage negative findings. While this didn't happen frequently, it happened more often as we went south, and by south I mean south of Columbus, Ohio. In both southern Ohio and Kentucky, EEOC investigators were sometimes followed by the proverbial pick-up truck with gun rack and silk-screened Confederate flag in the rear window. Fortunately, this only happened to me once.

To make better use of time, we'd usually have several cases with us on a weeklong trip. On one particular trip, I was in southern Ohio meeting with a union president in a motel room. He had two hulks, ostensibly "Communists" (whatever threat that signified), with him. During our meeting, he kept swinging a golf club. Each stroke landed closer and closer to my feet as he punctuated his strokes with a word finishing off with the following:

"This" (swing) "really" (swing) "pisses" (swing) "me" (swing) "off."

With all the above as context, that night I returned to my two-story motel, a generic painted cinder block economy motel building. All of the rooms had outside entrances, and I saw a guy backing out of my room with papers in his hand. We were civil, not criminal, investigators, but I was full of righteous ire. As I passed him on the second floor passageway, I grabbed his free arm in a hammerlock and threw him against the wall. I yelled, "Federal Agent! What the hell did you take out of my room?"

I then kicked his feet apart and pulled up on his arm. It was then that I realized that my arm was almost fully extended holding his wrist below his shoulders. He was close to a foot taller than I. Moreover, all he had to do was back up and I'd have been over the rail. It was a tiger by the tail situation.

Luckily for me, he was stunned. He stammered, "I, I'm the Assistant Manager and was just taking inventory. I didn't take anything, honest."

Instantly, the pounding in my red face and neck became embarrassment instead of ire. What a dumb ass I was. I released him and muttered, "Okay" and he hustled away. He didn't seem to notice he was twice my size. He wasn't on duty the next morning when I checked out, and I told no one what had happened for many years. In my defense, I can only say that I was younger than twenty-five at the time. Of course, on the other hand, so are many military and police officers, whom we never wish to let get away with such behavior even under real threat.

*****

Chas, the District Director, liked to brag to industry groups that he burned his people out in two years. My father, who was in HR, heard him say this in one of his speeches. I lasted only two years because I left for another promotion. I stayed in the federal EEO field though.

The DOD

Each department within the government had its own rules and policies. For instance, I thought the training period at EEOC was too short, but the DOD's training was virtually nonexistent. At EEOC, we mostly dealt with individual complaints. At the DOD, we were given free rein in the form of general equal opportunity reviews to review the employment systems of facilities. Further, there might be ten of thousands of employees in each review, and if needed, we would require corporate-wide changes.

Personally, it was heady work for a person in his mid-twenties.

My office partner was a year and a half younger than I, and cocky. For example, he was once asked, having shown up alone, if he intended to do a major (read: several thousand person facility) review by himself. His response was that he was reminded of the Texas Ranger's reply when he showed up alone to squelch a riot. "One riot. One ranger," said the ranger.

Whenever he was asked to write of his accomplishments, he did a great job. When he was complimented for this, he'd say, "It is a sick dog that won't wag its own tail."

He once reviewed a small factory in which he found that if an employee produced over quota, he/she would receive bonus pay; however, there was an unwritten rule in which everyone on his team had the opportunity to punch him *once* on the upper arm. The idea was to make the arm sore enough so that the hot shot worker wasn't able to break quota again. Management turned a blind eye to the practice.

*****

It was our job to ensure equal treatment, not fair treatment. There is a difference. We often heard "but it's not fair" when we turned down a complainant or found for a company. It wasn't politically correct, but I often told an employer, "We don't care if you beat your employees, but if you do, we monitor the strokes to ensure equal treatment." Sometimes I followed it up with the statement that I assumed the local police *would* have a problem if you beat your employees. This was generally added if I was feeling sensitive or if I felt that the company looked like it had been given a free pass.

The *equal, not necessarily fair* rule meant that we saw many crazy human resource policies that we had no business commenting upon. If an investigator paid attention, he or she got quite an education about HR. It was not uncommon for a company's Human Resources or Equal Opportunity representative to "explain" why this or that policy was, by far, the best way to go on some employment issue, only to find a conflicting, but equally defended, policy at a nearby competitor's.

On the other hand, when I was a supervisor, there were two common types of complaints received from companies and/or universities. The first was that one of my employees had commented negatively on some policy that had no EEO impact. If it were true, this was a valid complaint.

The other complaint, which was invalid, was that EEOC (DOD,HEW, or DOL) didn't have the right to review HR policies or treatment of a particular group of employees or titles because we *couldn't* understand the intricacies of the job. This would be seen most often at universities. The deans or chairpersons felt that it was improper to have to explain to someone outside their field why a woman was not granted tenure while a male with equal credentials was. For example, many EEOC employees had degrees in the social sciences, but they didn't need to understand particle physics to determine whether there was a case of unfair treatment (in the physics department). We weren't judging the quality of the department; we just wanted to understand what standards were in place for everyone's treatment.

A review of equal treatment is much easier to do in a class or group situation in which the examination of at least several people (of one gender or one race) is compared against a larger group (of the opposite gender or a different race). Admittedly, this equal treatment policy review is not as easy to understand in a one-on-one situation.

Once, I was investigating the firing of an advertisement agency's account manager. The agency claimed that the man was fired for incompetence. When I first met with three or four company reps, I was told that the guy they fired wanted to name a stove "The Lion of the Kitchen". At this point, they all laughed and sat back as if investigation was over. Unfortunately, they were talking to someone who doesn't get ads, and to me "The Lion in the Kitchen" isn't any sillier than many other slogans I've heard.

Some DOD cases

I reviewed a small foundry in which the EEO Director wore many "hats"; he was also the Safety Director, Labor Relations Manager, and Sales Manager. The furnaces were very small and were accessed through small grated doors into which men inserted long tongs into the furnace to pull the pieces out. The place was not unlike a dozen blacksmith shops all in one place except that the product they were working with was aluminum. As we toured the place, I heard a shout, and "Safety Director" turned around, and then said, "Ha ha! The Union president just backed into a grate and burned his ass."

We continued on the tour and then returned to his office. At this point, over the P.A. system, an announcement came over the speakers into the offices and the plant. "Will the owner of Ohio license XYZ, please move your car? You are blocking the company ambulance."

I stood up, grabbed my keys, and, as I headed for the door, told the man "of many hats", "Sorry; that's my car. I'll move it, but I never saw the ambulance when I parked there."

"It's just an unmarked '59 Chevy wagon we put a mattress in. We have so many accidents here," he said.

Such was life before OSHA really took hold.

*****

Sometimes, companies surprised me. In 1973, the U.S. participation in Viet Nam was winding down. At the same time, I was at a large earthmoving manufacturer, but the HR Director told me about a second part of the facility of which I was unaware. We drove out of the small city through farmland to a site that had many acres. Upon these acres sat row upon row of large, rusting earthmovers. The director explained that these were part of a four hundred million dollar, multi-year contract. The company had built them with bulletproof windows and camouflage paint. (In 1973, that sum of money bought a lot more than it does now.) However, the army neglected to buy spare parts, so when the equipment was ready to be shipped, the company was told to wait. That's when the company moved the equipment out to the field and started charging rent.

According to my host, "the government has already paid for the earthmovers, but doesn't want them now. They are selling them to whomever wants to pop out the bulletproof windows, scrape, and repaint them." However, since any other purchaser (except this company) would have to pay shipping, the company won the bid to buy back its own pre-paid equipment at rock-bottom prices. Moreover, it was taking the government so long to process the purchase that the company was told to keep charging the rental fees month after month.

Although he knew it wasn't my job to report this situation, he told me, "Anything you could do would be appreciated." The company had already written the local congressman a *"stop us before we kill again"* letter, but to no avail.

*****

On one review I discovered that in addition to women being forbidden to do "heavy" work, men were forbidden to do "close" work that required manual dexterity. When I pointed this out to the personnel director, he told me that no man could do close work. This review coincided with the end of the era that women had trouble getting into medical school, especially specializing in surgery. My response to him was that I hoped he never needed brain surgery because he'd have a hard time finding a woman neurosurgeon to do the "close" work.

*****

Reviews could, from the start, seem to raise an equal employment issue, but then could end up very off-the-wall and memorable, but less than terribly interesting from an EEO perspective. This was the case of the paint manufacturer who hired chicken sexers.

In 1973 I was reviewing the research division of a large paint manufacturer. I noticed the company employed a high percentage of Asians technicians. This particular division was located in a suburb of a large city that normally would employ no more than two percent Asian employees; however, in this case approximately thirty-five to forty percent of the technicians were Asian. I was still in my "Aha!" mode since this happened in the first ten years of EEO enforcement, and I quickly decided to find out what the company was doing (or what they were trying to get away with). Even after the first seven years of EEO I had not learned that when things were really out of whack, there was usually a benign explanation such as data entry error. After those first few years of civil rights law, real group discrimination was usually more subtle than an absolute zero female, minority utilization, or minority promotion, or as seen in this case, minority representation many times higher than predicted or expected.

When I asked the company representative what the technicians did at the facility, I was told that the technicians matched the paint samples on consumer's plasticized strips with the color seen on the dried wall after painting. (Software paint matching programs did not yet exist.) He further explained that the reason for the high percentage of Asian employees had to do with the hiring of Japanese chicken sexers. It was obvious from his enjoyment of the situation that he had had to explain this before.

I said, "Okay, I'll bite. Answer the three obvious questions. What is a "chicken sexer"? Why are they Japanese? What does this have to do with paint samples?"

His answers:

1) Chicken sexers are highly trained and valued people who determine the gender of chickens at birth so that either feed will not wasted on males who are to be discarded or that the wrong type of feed will not be wasted on the wrong gender as different feed is given to those raised for meat (males) or those raised to produce eggs. Gender difference in chicks is apparent to most only five or six weeks after birth, while chicken sexers can tell after a day or so. The ability to determine proper feed usage five or six weeks earlier is very valuable.

2) Historically, a small segment of Japanese society has trained, and practiced, and passed tests on how to do chicken sexing more than any other culture. Japanese chicken sexers are valued in many countries. (This is as true today in a few countries as it was when this occurred.)

3) Matching exact color or perceiving the slightest color difference is something the company felt chicken sexers could do a lot better than anyone else. Thus, we hired quite a few Japanese chicken sexers to match paint colors."

At this point, I didn't need anything more from an equal opportunity perspective, but my host added an interesting twist. He told me that in the previous year the samples had been "just a little bit off", and the company could not figure out the reason why. Then they noticed something. Their windows faced north, and a hundred yards northeast stood the town's water tower.

The previous year the water tower had been painted, presumably by the high school seniors, with the local school colors of orange and black. The reflections of these colors from the water tower into the windows of company defeated the best efforts of the Japanese chicken sexers/technicians. That is, until a city employee climbed the tower and re-painted it to its original color of white.

If my reports justifying the high Asian employment at this defense contractor were ever read, I hope the reader found them amusing (more about reports being read in another section).

*****

Most of the more bizarre stories I am relating occurred in the early days of EEO. Prior to my becoming a manager, I experienced many of these things, but once I was promoted I didn't hear of the crazy stuff going on probably because those under me (or other managers) felt they might get into trouble relating them. I am including a few more of my pre-management stories here.

In the training of EEOC and DOD employees, we had an unwritten policy of "it goes without saying". However, all too often we found that although it might be considered insulting to their intelligence, it *really* needed to be said or should have been. Of all the rules we had *The Do-not-touch-the-company-representative* rule ranked near the top. We also used the generic name of *Mr. Contractor* for training purposes.

Homero Gonzalez was a very nice guy as well as a conscientious employee. However, once I took Homero with me on a case, and we had reached an impasse with the HR manager who had declared that the union wouldn't agree. Homero got up, walked over to the representative, and giving him a crushing hug on the shoulders, said, "Don't worry, Mr. Contractor. They are good Christian gentlemen in the Union. They will agree." The HR manager looked at me with terror as if I needed to call my Doberman off. Did I fail to mention another unspoken rule: Never use religion to argue with company representatives!

*****

There were also cases with unintended consequences. When we demanded that women who merited it be allowed to be linemen, AT&T agreed. As a result, they also opened up the job of telephone operators to men. Soon, 2% of linemen were women, and 25% of operators were men.

In another case, an auto manufacturer opened heavy jobs to women. Afterwards, because of this, many a male heart attack victim, who wished for light duty, used his seniority to move to the previously all-female job of seat sewing. Yes, there was a time prior to the use of robotics when areas of car seats were partially hand-sewn.

*****

Then there was Lou, with whom I worked at EEOC and DOD, and then later supervised at DOL.

Once while at DOD, we went to do joint reviews of two large auto plants. He was to be the lead investigator on one, and I, the lead on the other. As we opened the first review, the corporate rep. from Detroit appeared. While this rep was always obnoxious, he felt a particular need to goad Lou. So when Lou talked, he put his feet on the desk facing Lou.

However, when it is the corporate rep's turn to talk, Lou would shield himself by opening his briefcase so that rep couldn't see him, either. If the rep moved to get a better view, Lou would put his head deeper into the briefcase.

The local HR Director motioned me into the hall. As we stood there, he said, "This is insane. We actually have a good story to tell." We decided, though, to let the two antagonists have their fun and went off to do the review on our own.

*****

Bill, my office partner, and I were to do another joint review at the divisional headquarters of a Fortune 100 firm. That morning, he drove his government-issued car to pick me up. As I stumbled bleary-eyed out of my home, I didn't notice that we were wearing identical tan London Fog coats. If I had noticed, I wouldn't have cared since approximately 50% of all male office workers wore them in the northern half of the country during the winter.

We arrived at the company, and were greeted by our host, who directed us to hang up our coats in a closet near his office. After doing so, we turned and entered the conference room to start the review with the five company representatives. At this, our host gasped, "Oh my God!" He continued with, "Now, they are issuing them uniforms." It turned out that our identical coats covered identical navy blue blazers, charcoal pants, wingtips, white oxford cloth button-down shirts, and identical red and blue striped ties. I guess the FBI wasn't the only agency where the G-men dressed the same.

*****

With regard to the behavior of co-workers, one of my most embarrassing moments occurred at a plant in Lorain,

Ohio. I was the third reviewer to go to the facility. At the "closeout" meeting in which I was explaining to the HR Director what had been found, I noticed that he let me talk. However, he went on with his other business of reading, writing, and going to the file cabinet for more files.

Finally, I said, "Hello, I'm here!"

He looked up and said, "Oh, you are serious."

I said, "Of course, what did you think?"

To which he said, "Well, your two predecessors weren't serious. The first one lectured me on Ohio history, and the second one invited me to see what a great car he had for a federal employee. It was an old Lincoln ragtop with rips and beer cans in the back seat. They didn't talk at all about how we were doing with EEO."

The reviewer, that lectured that local manager about Ohio history, but completely neglected to discuss the company's EEO situation, was an attorney. I also suspected he continued to regularly abuse alcohol. When we had our quarterly (local) general staff meetings at DOD, there was an inevitable reminder to act "professionally" at all times. It was then, and only then, when our attorney/historian would rouse himself from his stupor and pipe up to say, "Only attorneys and physicians are 'professionals'. I'm the only professional here."

However, he didn't exhibit his professional behavior when he was in the field. Even when he was in his own office, he could do strange things. Once, this "professional" felt the need to show his disdain for the negotiations going on in the next office, which shared thin walls. He turned on, at full volume, a repeating laugh-track, locked his office door, and then went to lunch.

I have to say, though, that I (and two other colleagues) felt that these quarterly meetings had, over time, become a "necessary evil" because of some the administrative non-sense that went on. We even developed a system between ourselves whenever it became too much. One or the other of us would surreptitiously raise two curled fingers of one hand and wiggle them like antennae, then "tune" them toward the speaker. To us, this was the "Automatic B.S. detector". Very funny, I thought. On the other hand, I didn't realize that years later this nonsense would come back and bite me.

Why It is Called the Rust Belt

For years, economists and politicians alike have been talking about how we "lost" the auto, steel, and tiring manufacturing in the area. How can we compete with low wage, overseas companies in what has been called "a race to the bottom"? Isn't management as responsible as labor when both sides have to sign the contract?

At DOD I had three close-up views of what went wrong. All are, admittedly, anecdotal.

1. Once, I was walking through an automobile plant with the head of the local HR department when I saw an employee sitting and reading *War and Peace*, the penultimate long novel. It gave him something to do while waiting. His job on the assembly line was dropping a foam seat insert into the front driver's side of the cars that had bucket seats. Since most of the cars of this model didn't have bucket seats, he just sat and waited until the correct color code came through that would trigger his dropping of the one pound foam insert. It was the easiest job I ever saw.

Further down the assembly line, I saw a man down in a pit that the cars rolled over. As they passed, he reached up with a heavy pneumatic gun and added about twelve bolts to each car. His "gun" forearm was noticeably larger than the one he didn't use to apply the bolts. Jokingly, I asked the HR Manager what great crime the man in the pit had committed to be assigned such a job. He told me that this man was one of their best workers, and further, that the employee reading *War and Peace* was more typical and would never do the job in the pit. Both of these men, as well as all the other assembly line workers, were paid the exact same hourly rate.

He went on to tell me that the plant had to be staffed at 120% because of absenteeism. His classic example of this need for replacement staff was the young employee who was called into his office because of his routine of missing a day every week. He asked the employee: "Why do you only come in four days a week?"

His answer: "Because I can't get by on just three (days' pay)."

2. On another occasion, during a tour of a large steel plant, the HR manager and I had to climb and then cross a steel walkway over what was called a sidewalk. This sidewalk was a road-sized ribbon, several inches thick, of hot steel going down a conveyor. Although it was winter, all the plant's windows were open because of the heat given off from the molten steel. As we continued across, we had to step over a man sleeping on the walkway. I asked the HR representative why he allowed something both so unsafe and non-productive. He said, "Shhh, he's a union steward. If I wake him, we'll just have trouble."

3. Finally, the tire industry. I sent someone down to do a review in the Akron tire plants. At this time tire plants still dominated Akron. He was to interview employees in the cafeteria because the company didn't want the employees off the job. While we didn't like restricted access to employees, the rubber plants had a rule that made it necessary. Once an employee made his quota, he could stop work and still get his eight hours' pay. However, he couldn't go home. On the other hand, no one wanted to do extra work be-

cause that would reduce the potential for overtime. So, everyone tended to finish by 1:30 or 2:00 in the afternoon, and would drift down to the cafeteria to wait for the 3 o'clock whistle that let them go home.

The Sex Experts

At DOD we reviewed federal contractors as well as investigated some complaints. The vast majority of investigators at DOD were male. Most of them, especially the older males, neither liked gender cases nor wanted to deal with them. Therefore, my partner Bill and I got all the sex discrimination complaints, and were jokingly called the *sex experts*. As an aside, companies are prohibited from engaging in *sex* discrimination when what is meant is discrimination due to gender. The word *sex* is used, inappropriately, in all the civil rights laws. The reason *sex* continues to be used when *gender* is meant is that the relevant laws and Executive Orders use the word *sex*.

But a bit of history first to explain more fully why these older, male investigators didn't like sex cases. First, they felt that by adding sex to Title VII (of the 1964 Civil Rights Act), it just watered down civil rights, which was intended for blacks. There was some truth to this, even if it sounds politically incorrect. Because the women's movement was weak in the early sixties, it didn't have the power to put gender into the prohibited cases for discrimination. Rather, in exchange for "yes" votes, Southern Democrat senators put *sex* into the 1964 Civil Rights Act to water it down. This can be verified by looking at the record of debate on the floor of the Senate.

The enforcement of civil rights under Title VII by the federal government didn't really start until 1966. The '64 law took effect in July '65, but without an investigator cadre to call upon, staffing took place slowly. So, at DOD, retired military officers who understood bureaucracy, but not civil rights, came in and minority activists and ministers, who knew civil rights, but not how industry works, joined them. I started in 1969. At that point in time, for training purposes, every single decision of the EEOC could be read in a few weeks. The state female weight-lifting laws weren't even invalidated until 1972. In the first few years, some companies with male-only and female-only titled jobs changed the names to Operator "A" and Operator "B" positions, and got away with it for awhile. For many years, almost no one with HR or business experience was hired by the government EEO investigative agencies.

One of the benefits of being deemed a *sex expert* was that I was assigned big gender cases because almost nobody else at the DOD wanted them. The best example involved a facility that employed 25,000 workers. It was part of what was then one of the top ten companies based on employment size in the U.S.

I went to the fired employee's house to investigate and, as a result, got a graphic demonstration of how our case backlog delayed our getting to cases. In this case, the charge was, "they fired me for being pregnant."

A little girl answered the door, looked at me, and yelled, "Mommy, there is a man here for you." This child was the one the woman had, allegedly, been fired for carrying.

The facts were uncontested. If an employee had fewer than four years' seniority and a layoff occurred while the employee was on short-term medical leave, the seniority applied except in the case of short-term leave for pregnancy. If the leave was due to pregnancy, seniority was irrelevant, and the employee would then be the first to be laid off. For example, a man with a year of seniority, who shot himself in the foot deer hunting, kept his seniority while he was recuperating if a layoff was announced. However, a woman with three and a half years of seniority at home on pregnancy leave lost her seniority in the case of layoffs and, effectively, became the first to be out the door. By the time of my investigation, more than 400 women at this facility alone had lost their jobs because of this policy.

After we attempted and failed to get the company to settle the case, I wrote it up and had it sent forward to Washington for review and approval so that we could send this "no brainer" to our lawyers for enforcement. In due course, the review came back. After an introduction, the reviewer copied my write up word for word for ten pages until it came to the final paragraph. Even then, all but one word was the same. The reviewer added "not" after "therefore" and in front of "guilty".

I called our headquarters, hoping there was some mistake. After all, not a bit of my reasoning was disputed; not a bit of reasoning was added. I finally got hold of the Washington bigwig who *wrote* the opinion, but all I got was the run around. There wasn't any reason he could name to overturn the case. He just talked in circles. The case was closed. The rejection came from the highest levels and even my boss could not appeal the decision. Besides that, he told me it was just a *sex case*.

That should have been the end of the story except that several months later, the largest companywide EEO case settlement in the country to date was announced. It was the same large corporation that I had dealt with in the pregnancy layoff case. With this agreement, many gender issues were settled. One clause in the settlement stood out. Although no one who had been previously shafted by the pregnancy layoff clause would get her job back, this policy was, henceforth, dropped nationwide. It turned out that the chief negotiator for the government was the same person who had denied approval of my case earlier.

I got to know him well over the ensuing years. He eventually confirmed that he had used dropping my case as the final carrot to the company in order to get a nation-wide settlement of a much broader scope.

While it is true that the settlement didn't help any of 400+ affected women at my complainant's facility and while it is also true that the settlement broke new ground on a wide scale for female employees nationwide, I have several questions for readers to ponder.

Was it right to trade my case for the settlement? Is the bestest for the mostest right, generally? All the time? Never?

DOD Administration

Government administration can be goofy, in my opinion, but having worked for these five agencies/departments (IRS, EEOC, DOD, HEW, and DOL), I thought that the DOD was clearly the least goofy. Nonetheless, I once saw in a copier room at the DOD, the following sign:

In case of major fire, call Papenfuss. In case of minor fire, call Smith.

Next to each name was the phone extension and a regulatory cite so that the rules could be looked up to determine when a fire was *major* enough to call Papenfuss or *minor* enough to call Smith.

While I felt that working for the Defense Department was the best, administratively, we were civilians doing the work of EEO, and thus, didn't really fit in. Those officers in the business of contracting for the latest tank or desiring the bullet specs to fly through the vetting process couldn't understand why we stood in the way over something they couldn't see as having anything to do with the DOD's mission.

*****

Once, a general came through our office to review us. We were to stand in our doorways as he walked through looking at four floors' worth of civilian office employees. No one was allowed to address him, and I always figured this poor guy had to be bored to death. His first stop was to present Dick O'Reilly with a certificate for not using any of his sick leave for three years. Dick, ironically, wasn't there; he'd broken his leg skiing and was on sick leave.

As he passed our Deputy's office, Mo said, "I see you came up through the Marines. Did you have the operation?" The aides looked horrified. A civilian had spoken.

"What operation?" asked the general.

"I was a Navy captain," said our Deputy. "I heard that before you can be a Marine general, they have to drill a hole in your head and pour cement in."

I never looked to see if any aides wet their pants over this, but after a beat or two, the general roared with laughter, went over, grabbed Mo, and they went into his office and shut the door. The aides stood outside while, for the next half hour or so, all we heard were the sounds: mumble mumble HAR! HAR! mumble mumble (The pair sounded like pirates from an old Errol Flynn movie.)

*****

DOD Clericals

I once asked a friend, who was a former fed, what he missed most and least about the government. I think his answer would be typical. He missed the security. He had left government work to go into a private practice of law in order to support his family. He said he didn't miss "having to kiss a secretary's ass to get anything done." However, since personal computers (PCs) came into use, that crude sentiment wouldn't ring true even though federal employees didn't get PCs until ten years after everyone else.

Federal clerical support was very uneven. There wasn't any federal locality pay, yet. The private pay rate for clerical support varied by city. Nonetheless, Cleveland DOD, in spite of highly competitive pay, generally had weak clerical support while Cleveland HEW had great clerical support.

Once, early on at DOD, I took an extremely important letter back to be retyped because the word *prescribed* was typed instead of the word *proscribed.* Her response to me was: "It wasn't my fault because the shorthand form for *pre* and *pro* are the same, and you didn't tell me which it was." I said I wasn't assigning fault to anyone, but needed the letter corrected. Tina refused to retype it, and was backed by my boss. He gave the retyping of the letter to another secretary rather than anger the original typist. Of course, this wouldn't have happened in the last fifteen to twenty years with the advent of word processing programs.

I dealt with this same typist for two years, speaking with her at least ten times a day. One day, having just left the office, I had the occasion to call my boss from the lobby. When she answered, I said, "Hi Tina. It's me. Can you let me talk to Dan?"

She said, "Who is calling, please?"

Frustrated at not being recognized, I said, "It's an angry congressman."

At this point, Dan comes on the line. I said, "Hi Dan. It's Chuck. I just..." and he cut me off with a quite-serious...

"Can't talk right now, I've got an angry congressman on the line."

*****

DOD Reports

The worst case I ever saw of phony reports happened while I was working at DOD. I was never in a supervisory position at DOD; however, the fact that everyone in the office was aware of this matter is what makes it worse.

We had one really fast reviewer/investigator. He had recently been transferred to a sub-office, which was still under our office's supervision. From the Pentagon, it was announced that in three months, they'd be coming to do a general review of all our files and systems. That set off a scramble to see if there was anything we had to worry about.

In the course of the scramble, the reports of our "superstar" were looked at. We had a standard 25-page report that we filed on every case. The front page contained general contract, employment and identifying information. The back page carried the number of hours involved and the investigator's signature as well as the signatures of the supervisor and manager that signed off on the report, after having found it to be complete and of good quality. The guts of the report were found in the middle 23 pages.

First one, then two, and then all of the "superstar's" reports were discovered to be blank except for the first and last pages.

At this point, how does one fire or discipline Mr. Superstar? To do so, one would have to admit that neither the Deputy nor the Director ever read any of Mr. Superstar's files. And if his weren't read, what makes anyone think that anyone else's files were ever read, complete or not?

It was the beginning of summer and we had three months to prepare. The solution became obvious. The Director was hiring a college student to be a summer intern. This intern was assigned to spend his summer going through the files and filling in the blanks. He had no knowledge as to the right answers to the questions posed in those pages, but then, neither did the auditors. All that mattered was that the blanks were filled in. Occasionally, he had to write descriptive sentences, too. They couldn't be apparent nonsense, but they didn't have to be true, either. Every week or so a senior employee would check to see if the blocks that were checked, the sentences and paragraphs written, and the statistics presented were all plausible. When the contents of a given report were deemed plausible, it was re-filed so the auditors could review it. And I thought my intern experience at the IRS was strange!

At the end of the summer we gave the intern a farewell party. When one of the more senior members of the staff heard about the party, he was said to have grumbled, "Party??? That kid should never be allowed to leave the office alive with what he knows!"

*****

After spending a couple years at DOD, I got a call from the woman who had been one of my supervisors at EEOC. She offered me a promotion and a job at HEW. For those who may not remember HEW and think that nothing in the federal government goes away, I have both good news and bad news. The good news: HEW went out of business. The bad news: HEW became the Department of Education *and* the Department of Health and Human Services.

HEW

Title IX

Today, and for many years, Title IX has been synonymous with women in athletics. Although I have been accused of being both jaded and anti-female in my dotage, having lived through the early days of Title IX, I have a different perspective. I'm not anti-female. In fact I filed and won a case on behalf of my daughter. More on that later.

I just don't believe that things are as bad as they were prior to the early seventies. One of my favorite cartoons of the era (I think it is a 'Tank McNamara') pictures a reporter in a broom closet with the women's athletic director who is sitting behind a card table with a deflated basketball. The reporter has apparently asked what the women's AD would do with a bigger budget because the caption on the cartoon is as follows:

"Well, for one thing I'd buy a new basketball."

That cartoon wasn't far off—for 1975.

The key parts of Title IX are only three paragraphs long. One paragraph exempts the military academies from having to admit women. There are now women who've gone through the academies and their whole military career, been promoted to general or admiral, and subsequently retired since the academies decided to admit women.

One paragraph says that single sex colleges can exist, but if they do admit women, the women must be treated the same as men.

The final paragraph basically says to treat males and females the same in every way.

Athletics was a small, small part of (the original) Title IX. Before 1973, it was legal to refuse to admit women to medical school, law school, business school. If they *were* admitted, limits could be put on the number of admissions, and they could be treated differently than their male counterparts. Even after 1973 it was only federal funding that could be denied if violations of Title IX occurred. For several years post-1973, we had to work out what "don't discriminate" meant in practice. I worked in the area of civil rights for several years before Title IX. So, when it hit and took effect, I got to lead a team that wrote guidelines and be involved in the first cases. It was a rush! We accomplished a lot quickly.

I went to the University of Minnesota for a conference regarding the "new" Title IX.

EEO/AA Directors reported directly to CEOs and presidents at that time; now they generally report to the HR director and, as a result, have much less power in their organization than before. While there, I met Lillian Williams, who was in charge of all university-related issues regarding equal employment or equal education. She told me that the state legislature had offered her four million dollars to get the university into Title IX compliance, but she turned them down.

"Do you want to know why?" she asked me.

"Of course," I said.

"You people don't have your act together yet. You don't know what you want us to do. If I spend four million dollars guessing what we need to do and guess wrong, I'll lose the goodwill of the legislature when I go back for more money."

Lillian Williams, now deceased, was one smart lady!

*****

One of the earliest issues of Title IX was the following: co-ed contact sports or not? With girls wrestling on boys' teams and with some female place kickers around now, this must seem archaic. Nonetheless, a decision had to be made early on as to whether women should be melded into men's teams or not. Woody Hayes of *The* Ohio State University said we should let women come out for football. "My boys would kill them," he's quoted as saying. He was a class act all the way, that Woody.

At first a major women's group demanded that basketball rules inherently made it a non-contact sport. Then I was told that Dr. Betty Johnson, who is also known as Bunny Johnson, was taken to a Washington Bullets' (now they go by the more sensitive name of Washington Wizards) game. She was seated in the front row. Apparently, some giant covered in flop sweat flew into her during the game, and the women's group decided basketball was a contact sport.

My Daughter's Case

In 1978, when Michelle entered fifth grade, we found that her school required all girls to embroider their names on the back of their gym suit, and all boys to put their names on with indelible marker. To quote Michelle, "I'm not into domestics." I made what I thought would be a quick phone call to the school to ask them to drop this rule they'd obviously forgotten to drop. I was told that the rule had always been that way. (I have learned that whenever I hear "it's always been that way", what is meant is "it is going to stay that way.") When I said that the rule violated federal law and could cause the school system to lose millions in aid, those in charge said, "What are you going to do? Make a federal case of it?"

Because I only handled Higher Education cases, I called my office for the persons responsible for Elementary and Secondary Education cases. I told them I had an easy one for them that they could knock out in a few hours and get a win.

They called the school administrator and got the same brush off that I had gotten. Then they sent the school system a letter finding against them, effectively threatening to take millions of dollars away. The school board counsel called; the rule was dropped; and almost everyone went away happy.

Early Title IX Cases

Early Title IX cases could be as mind-bendingly weird as the early Title VII cases had been at EEOC. Both types were often cases of first impression. Previously, no one had been able to complain successfully about certain types of mistreatment. When first impression complaints were made, the management's or university administration's reaction could often be summarized as "Huh?"

The team rep for a Big Ten women's swim team complained of mistreatment. She conceded that the women had their own pool. So, what could be the problem? An investigator went to the school and saw the men's pool. Then he went to the lower level of the same building to see the women's pool. In order to support the weight of the water in the men's pool, there were pillars in the women's practice pool. Not only that, but the pillars were in the lanes, no less!

First, we had to point out to the athletic department that there was a problem. It was always preferable if the institutions being investigated suggested a remedy to their own problem. The athletic department could not, for the life of them, figure how to work out this problem. We paused (hint, hint). Then we asked if the men's program practiced over six hours a day. We were told no to that, and again we paused. They still didn't see how the problem could be solved, but the University Counsel, after he finished rolling his eyes, figured out how to split the usage time.

*****

We didn't find for all complainants. While we may have been sympathetic and some situations were politically incorrect, they weren't necessarily illegal.

All Big Ten universities have marching bands. Nine of the Big Ten schools were in my region. (This was when the conference could count to ten, and before the Big Ten Conference became eleven, now twelve universities, but I digress.)

Our office received a complaint that one of the schools was discriminating against the disabled and women in the marching band. Before the Americans with Disabilities Act, there was a handicap nondiscrimination rule covering federal contractors and grantees (also known as Section 503 and Section 504).

The school sent us a picture of the marching band that clearly showed there was female participation. The handicapped issue still needed to be resolved; however, to qualify for coverage here required that the person would have to be able to perform the duties. The school said, and then proved, that even if a person wasn't a Music major, he/she could still be in the band if there was a (Music major not required) opening.

In this case, the position available was the bass drum, but the student complainant was so obese that her stomach and drum together blocked her line of sight. Because of this, she kept running into the person in front of her.

*****

HEW's Office for Civil Rights had several ex-religious employees. For example, there was Beth, the ex-Mother Superior. Before joining our staff, she had been a cocktail waitress while working on her Ph.D. work in English. From there, she came to our office, doing the same type of work as we did. Further, she was married to an ex-priest who also worked with us. All of us were friends. Eventually, she ended up succeeding me in my Higher Education Regional Director role. I asked her once why she had left the convent. She said, "I was tired of all that humility crap." It's probably a good thing she left.

Working at Cleveland's Office for Civil Rights, there was a former Monsignor who was married to a former Mother Superior. Both of them reported to a man whose last name was Pope. They switched professions, but still reported to the Pope?

Akmed M. Stories

Akmed M. was both an artist and a lawyer. He received his law degree from one of the best law schools in the United States, and his Ph.D. in Art from a school in South Asia where his father was president, and Akmed Junior sat on its board of trustees.

I think I first heard about Akmed in his complaint against Super State. He had been hired for one year as an Assistant

Professor in Art, but his contract wasn't renewed. To his way of thinking, it was a clear case of national origin discrimination.

This led, separately, to a federal court trial and an investigation by me. Among Akmed's reported accomplishments during his one year at Super State were the following:

He had a Sunday afternoon indoor *Art Happening* on campus. He charged one dollar (no change and no fives or tens, please). He then took the box office receipts, lit them, broke an egg in a frying pan, and fried the egg in the heat of the dollars. Count the laws and school rules this violated.

He had an *Art in motion* project. He told his students to look up at exactly 10:00 am in the courtyard of one of the tall SSU buildings. When they looked, he peed into the sunlight, and they got to see urine twinkling in the sunlight all the way down. This event took place in the art department in the "anything goes" early '70s, which may be the only reason I can think of for not firing him for that stunt.

The chair of his department gave him a place to stay as well as rides to school. Nonetheless, one day as classes were changing and students were everywhere, Akmed and the chairman were walking in the main area of SSU. They disagreed about the rights and wrongs of the East and West Pakistan War (that's how Bangladesh came into being). From Akmed's point of view, the chairman was wrong so he threw him down the steps and screamed, "You, Sir, are a cur!"

Akmed went to Columbus for an art show that he mistakenly thought was to be devoted completely to his works. When he found out he was wrong, and further that he was only allotted a corner section in which to display his art, he left his works boxed up. As I recall, he put up a sign that read, "These boxes contain works too much for the eyes of modern man!" The sign, by the way, won an award.

Akmed sued the school when it didn't renew his contract. At one point in his trial in federal court, he excused himself, went to the restroom, cut himself slightly, and then put the blood on toilet paper. Then he returned to court and yelled, "You have wrung the very blood from me!"

I only read the transcript, but later in the trial, the Dean was asked for one reason he didn't renew Akmed's contract (forget peeing out a window, burning money, or throwing your supervisor down the stairs). He said that Akmed was too stuck on himself. When asked to illustrate, the Dean referred to the book *Akmed by Akmed* in which there is a picture of Queen Elizabeth and Akmed together. "So?" said the lawyer.

"Well," said the Dean, "the caption is: 'Queen Elizabeth meets Akmed.'"

*****

Before I close this story on Akmed, there's another story that needs relating. Akmed said that the school officials had admitted they'd discriminated. Akmed said that, if I questioned these officials, they'd admit it. I assembled five of the people, including his advocate, who attended the meeting, in the very room where this admission had supposedly occurred.

I said, "Akmed says you all admitted that SSU discriminated against him—true or false?"

They all said, "True," and some, except for his lawyer, even laughed.

"Okay, what's the deal?" I asked.

All of them including Akmed's advocate said I should note the ceiling to floor crank-out windows. They said that Akmed went to one and squeezed himself halfway out and said, "Admit you discriminated or I'll jump." That's why they had admitted they discriminated.

One of them added, "We should have let the bastard jump," which got him a glare from the University Counsel.

Per usual, I wrote up the case, and my boss issued it. Akmed apparently didn't realize who wrote the case up and didn't hold this against me at the time. By the time I was Regional Director for Civil Rights in Higher Education, the person who issues findings, he wrote to me as *Dear Dr. Duffy* in a complaint against the University of Notre Dame. The school had failed to hire him as either the Dean of the Law School or the Chair of the Art Department. To him, it didn't matter that neither job was open. Further, in his application for either of the two positions, he wrote a letter addressed to Father Hesburgh[*] as *Dear Bigot Hesburgh*. The letter went on to say that "you probably won't hire me because I believe in Islam." The letter ended with the closing, "Yours in Christ."

I found against Dr. Akmed, but the complaints kept coming. The letters addressed to *Dr. Duffy* became, over time, addressed to *Mr. Duffy*, then *Duffy*, and finally *Bigot Duffy*. Akmed filed at least forty complaints even though some of them were outside my six-state area.

He had so many accomplishments and degrees that whenever he signed a letter, his degrees, and title abbreviations would reach the right margin and then crawl up the right side of the page.

My last memory of him occurred when lawyers were first allowed to advertise in newspapers. There was a time when the practice of law was considered too genteel to be advertised. When the ban was lifted in Chicago, the bar association urged class and restraint. Akmed took out the first ad in the *Tribune*. It said: "Summer suit sale. Two for the Price of one."

---

[*] Father Hesburgh, former Chair of the United States Civil Rights Commission, was President of the University of Notre Dame at the time

Disability Cases

In addition to the marching band case, we did many other disability discrimination cases. Some of the things we did then are not considered politically correct now. However, it was more than thirty years ago, and we hadn't evolved as much as we have now.

I attended a policy conference with the (nine) other Higher Ed. Regional Directors. HEW General Counsel's learned staff (*learned* is a term for someone from Washington, even if they just got there) was going to explain the rules for the new Sections 503 and 504 of the '73 Rehab Act (the predecessor of the Americans with Disabilities Act). Over the three-day conference, they asked for questions. I asked if being fat was a handicap and whether being ugly was a handicap. I was partially serious and partially having fun with these questions.

Eventually we were told that fat and ugly aren't handicaps, but hideous and obese are. I asked how to recognize hideous and obese versus fat and ugly. I said that in the field these things weren't theory. We needed to know for casework. I was told that essentially hideous and obese were defined as *really* fat and *really* ugly. Further, I asked whether a person needed to be hideous **and** obese or just one or the other. When they told me to shut up and sit down, I didn't really hear them over the laughter of my co-conspirators. By the way, the answer is: Either hideous or obese will do.

*****

For those who are thinking that I may be completely insensitive, I know from experience that these distinctions and definitions do matter. At HEW, I had a rare, direct call from a United States Senator wanting to know who we thought we were telling a friend of his who should or shouldn't be his secretary. His friend was either the head of surgery or the head of cancer treatment (I forget which it was) at a large university hospital in the Senator's state.

The facts were thus: this physician's secretary had to undergo facial cancer surgery at his hospital. After the surgery her face was so scarred and deformed that he didn't want her greeting visitors. Her clerical skills were undiminished, though. He felt, however, that it just didn't look good to have her in the front office greeting people. Never mind that the woman needed the job to pay medical bills and provide insurance. Never mind that the woman's face looked the way it did as a result of surgery at his hospital. The senator's friend fired her without trying to, at least, accommodate the complainant by giving her a less visible job behind the scenes.

Ignoring the fine points of the regulation, I asked the senator if he could just ask the physician whether the facts were as I stated them. He agreed, which, I thought, was pretty classy for a senator talking to a low-level bureaucrat. I got a call back from an aide. He told me that the senator would not be bothering me any more, and that his friend would be bringing the complainant back to work soon.

*****

In those early days of disability rules, I'd often have to go to conferences where, regardless of what the program stated, I was expected to address the question: What does the government want us to do?

Almost always I was preaching to the choir. That is, those persons setting up, much less attending a conference, were already interested in complying with the rules of disability accommodation. I was an expert by virtue of my title only. At the time, I ran a regional unit of the government that among other things checked compliance of handicap rules (Section 504 of the Rehabilitation Act of 1973) for institutions of higher education in six states. We enforced Section

504, but had almost no training in handicap discrimination. There wasn't any case law. The Americans with Disabilities Act was still years away.

Deb McWright and I went to one conference. She was new to our office, but had worked for some time at a state agency that dealt with handicap accommodation. I was going to make a few general statements, and then I'd ask Deb to take over on specifics. Deb had walked with the aid of crutches since childhood. She was not only one of the youngest people in the room, but she was one of a very few with a visible handicap.

When she attempted to get on the stage, and only then, did we notice that the stage was all open stairs without railings. As the audience watched, and to the embarrassment of our well-meaning hosts, we had to help Deb up the stairs to the podium to speak. To her credit, she started with a matter-of-fact, "You asked me to talk on specific accommodations. Well, the first thing is you could get some railings for this stage." Then she laughed in a *"we are all in on the joke"* way. Talk about instant credibility and goodwill!

Fire Rules (Again)

As mentioned before (at DOD), whoever is in charge of fires is apparently *big magic* to the administrative staff in the government. At HEW, I had a corner office, which came with two phones—one black and one red. The red phone didn't work, but the black one did. No one seemed to know what the red phone was for. One time I had some fun negotiating with the president of one of the state universities in Illinois (Northern, Eastern, Western, or Southern—take your pick). He wanted to know what the red phone was for. I joked that it was my direct line to SAC Command, and if he didn't agree to settle, we'd wipe his school off the map. The lawyer went crazy. Luckily, the president just laughed.

The president and I got along fine after that; the lawyer and I, not so much.

One day the red phone rang. I found out it was a check of the fire notification system. So I reported "no fire", and the test was over.

Three days later, Hazel, the Regional Administrative Officer, came steaming into my office. "You answered the red phone!" she said.

"Yes, it's on my desk, and it rang. I had wondered what it was," I said.

Hazel yelled, "That's my phone. I'm the fire officer. You can't answer it."

I said, "Okay, didn't know that. Strange it's on my desk though."

She said, "It has to be in a corner office on each floor."

I said, "So, I should have called your office, and you could come and answer it?"

She said, "Well, I was on leave on Friday, but you still shouldn't answer it."

I said, "So we burn a little while you come over to answer it, but we burn a lot if you are on leave and no one answers it?" By now, I was tired of the game, but since Hazel also ordered the toilet paper, I tried to be nice.

At this point she said something to the effect that she thought I should never touch the phone no matter what and it wasn't going to be moved. That's when I made the big mistake. I told her, "I don't care what the hell you think, let me get back to work."

The grievance that she filed said, "He had used the word, *hell*, and she was a churchgoing woman. He had to apologize."

I wrote her that I was sorry I felt it was necessary to use the word, *hell*, when I talked to her. She was happy she'd won and the red phone on my desk never rang again. Several months later, she arranged to have it moved to her desk even though her office was the only non-corner office with a red phone. Hazel just stood at my office door, beaming, the day that the workers (yes, plural) came without notice to remove the phone.

More HEW Administration

When I transferred to HEW, my reimbursement check for the move to Chicago was slow in coming. When I asked why, I was told I had failed to certify that I had not moved any open bottles of *wine* or *live parakeets*. Not open bottles of booze! Not live birds, mind you…just wine or live parakeets!

*****

A few weeks later I got a complaint from a nuclear physicist who claimed that Angela Davis, the '60s radical, was trying to kill him. I suggested he call the Chicago police. This angered him! He wrote that he could make a nuclear bomb and I had better watch out. It wasn't long before everyone on the floor had heard about this letter. Eventually, I received another letter from the gentleman. The person at the front desk called and told me to come and open it. In the meantime the admin staff hid around the corner of the drywall just in case the letter *was* a nuclear bomb. This story was funnier before Oklahoma City and the Twin Towers.

In the federal buildings I worked in, as well as the non-federal building that housed the leased HEW space, we had instructions for taking bomb threats. We were to ask the caller about thirty questions and then make sure that we informed the person that bombs and bomb threats are crimes. That'd work well! Right?

*****

Liner In, Liner Out?

I don't know what category this story falls under, but I have always liked it. I had to do a walk-through of a large university hospital. The hospital administrator was to accompany me. This was ceremonial B.S. and we both knew it so we were going to waste as little time as possible on it. The administrator greeted me with, "Are you a liner-in or liner-out guy?"

I told him I didn't know what that meant. He said that whenever government people came through, the hospital representative asked if the fed wanted plastic liners in the wastebaskets for sanitary purposes or wanted them out for fire protection purposes. Both liner-in and liner-out were required at the same time by the government. I told him that it wasn't my area, and I wasn't going to report on it. Out of curiosity, I asked, "How do you handle the situation?"

The hospital chief told me that they keep liner in; but if a liner-out guy came through, a hospital employee ran ahead and took the liners out till the fed was gone. Sometimes it is embarrassing to work for the feds. Okay, a lot of times.

*****

A major university in Michigan ran into trouble when it was discovered that the people with the title of Assistant Cashier were all women except for one man. This man made many times over what the women did. At that time, if a company were to discriminate in regards to wages for women or minorities, it was only fifty cents to two dollars an hour difference. No one was so foolish as to pay the lone white male many times what everyone else made. Nonetheless my team, team leader, and the university officials in charge of first response to such issues elevated the issue to the university counsel, the president, and me. It took us a half minute to find out that the title of Assistant Cashier is both the title of the people who run the cash registers at the university bookstore as well as the one person, (who happened to be a man), who was the treasurer of the university. Luckily for me, the university was as embarrassed as I for the lack of communication at the lower level of the investigation.

*****

We did a review of a non-university hospital in which the investigator questioned the lack of minority nurses given the availability in the area. The HR director said, "Oh, that's because we only hire our own graduates." That meant that she was defending discrimination in hiring with discrimination in the nursing school admissions. So, the investigators checked. They found that the nursing school admitted plenty of minorities, and further that the hospital didn't even hire predominately from its nursing school.

There we had a case in which the employer admitted guilt and was wrong.

In contrast to my beginning, as I neared the end of my career, I found that the fun cases (other than the massive dollar settlements, mostly for compensation for professional level women) were the misunderstandings.

The Back Scholarship

One of my favorite cases was the *back scholarship* case. A Big Ten school gave full golf scholarships to the top five male golfers on their team, but none to the women golfers. The men's team finished in the middle of the pack in conference play while the woman who complained was the individual Big Ten champ that year.

Moreover, a pre-World War II student had been an early woman's pro golf star and had established a scholarship for women golfers. The money in the scholarship fund had been building; however, not a dime was ever paid out. The finding wasn't hard to make.

I recall the conversation in which I told the university. "You owe her a scholarship."

In response, the Counsel said, "She's graduated. So, nothing can be done."

Because of the law being in effect for four years, I said, "Give her four years of 'back scholarship' plus interest just as you would have to with back-pay in an employment situation."

"That has never been done. Why should we do it? We'll beat you at trial!"

"Maybe so. We'll see after the case pends a year or so, and you have to defend yourself in the press."

We got the agreement the next day. What I thought was really neat is that the victim became a pro golfer, and donated the back scholarship monies into the original women's scholarship fund, which the school finally started paying out.

We All Play with the Same Money

The truth of the matter is that we all play with the same money, and the cost of the remedy to an on-going problem comes back on the taxpayer. Consider that when the feds take an action against a state or local governmental entity on behalf of a victim (who is also a taxpayer), the penalties will be paid out of taxpayer money. This circular use of funds always seemed bizarre to me.

On the surface, penalties against private employers felt less strange in that the "victim" was not being recompensed out of public money. On second thought, however, there is not much difference. Private companies use their markets as their income source. Costs of litigation and findings are translated into higher prices for goods and services (which will be paid in the private sector by the taxpaying public). In short, it comes back on the taxpayer. Add into this circular argument that the victim, the federal investigator, and the private employers are taxpayers and are all a part of that swirling money pool that is the national economy. Weird, huh?!

Supervision Wasn't as Bad?

After I was promoted to Regional Director for Higher Education, I felt I was in a strange position. All policy, case, and legal supervision came out of Washington. However, for administrative purposes and for evaluations, I was to report to a general Regional Director by the name of Ted Hines. Of course, no evaluations were ever done in all the years I was in this position.

Ted had come up through the Elementary and Secondary Education section. He felt that HEW's Civil Rights efforts should, to quote him, "be directed to help black children and not rich, white women." By this he meant that we shouldn't be wasting our time on cases of discrimination based upon gender salary differences at universities. Fortunately, he didn't interfere much in the work I was doing in the Higher Education unit.

He was smart and clear about what he expected. If there were a hundred *Number One* priorities and he was asked what he *really* wanted emphasized, he'd tell you. In fact, once he told the other two unit heads and me that we had to ask ourselves one question every morning when we got up. The question was this: Can I make Ted Hines look good today? If the answer was no, we should just go back to bed. Clear enough?

Some More University Cases

There actually were more serious cases to be handled. In the 1970s women tended to graduate from college at an older age than men. Because of this, women applied to medical schools later. Many of the medical schools had entry age distinctions. State schools claimed they owed taxpayers more *physician years* and thus, an age cut-off for admissions was okay even if it disproportionately affected women. For a while that continued.

As a result of one of our cases, the Supreme Court ruled that private schools had no such defense. The barrier later became irrelevant at public schools because women began to graduate at the same age as men.

*****

I sent an investigator to southern Illinois on a complaint that blacks could not take flying lessons at the local community college. She was directed out of town to the local airport where the flying instructor worked. Because the charge was so absurd, the college made the unusual decision not to send a representative out with her to defend them.

When the investigator, a young black woman, arrived at the airfield, she asked about the charge. The flight instructor calmly told her that blacks were too stupid to learn to fly. (While this happened more than thirty years ago, it was still nearly thirty years *after* World War II and all the African American Tuskegee airmen.)

The investigator returned to the campus and reported the conversation to the president. Since the president couldn't believe it, he had the instructor come to the campus to see if the instructor would repeat what he'd said earlier. He did, and to everyone's credit, the man was fired on the spot, and the student got both an apology and free flying lessons.

*****

Another student filed a charge because his state school, located four miles from the old Confederacy, refused to allow a blacks-only rifle club. In the process of checking out his complaint, I asked if blacks were allowed to join the all-campus rifle club, and he said yes to that. I further asked if he thought an all-black rifle club might make the school admin nervous, but he dismissed me as just another racist-honky. Actually, he wasn't that nice.

This same student was also part of the group that wanted the makeup of cheerleader squads to be the same percentage of blacks as the student body. At the time the campus was nine percent minority, and one of the eight cheerleaders was black. I guess the complainants weren't math majors. This group also felt it was discriminatory not to have all-black dormitories.

*****

One northern state school had an all black custodial force with all white supervision. With a straight face, the in-house counsel told me, "The exclusive route to supervision is promotion."

In response, also with a straight face, I asked him, "Has the university med school perfected the race transplant?"

*****

Single sex honorary societies supported by the university are illegal. We moved against one, and then found out from both the school and Washington that the President of the United States was a graduate of the college as well as a member of that honorary society, and we were to back off.

*****

When I was still a team member (and yet not Regional Director), we reviewed a prestigious private university. During the entrance conference, the president of the university, who later became a high-ranking United States cabinet member, couldn't hide his disdain for us. He told us that a negative finding would "most discommode," that he was no misogynist, that faculty vitae weren't fungible, that the school never had vacancies but would always hire the number one person in the world in any field at any time. After some more pompous talk, he told us he "welcomed our auditory function."

My boss, a well-educated, normally well spoken black woman, couldn't take it any more.

Her normal speech was as cultured as can be, but, to this man, her response in an Aunt Jemima-style voice was, "You doe'n worry honey, we gonna stick to you like white on rice." Then she looked at him and smiled. Whether or not he understood he was being mocked, we never knew. I can't say that the review was fun, but I sure enjoyed her comeback.

She was once put on a two-stop five-hour flight from Chicago to Cleveland because "Jane said you wanted to leave as close to 6:00 p.m. as possible." Jane was a clerical worker who was promoted to an investigator before I took over the unit, and thus, I inherited her. When our whole team was out in the field, at dinners out, someone had to be designated to stay behind to prevent Jane from stealing all the tips.

*****

Two years after the fact, I heard this story when I met the provost on an airplane. A team leader of mine wouldn't get to the point in negotiation with another Big Ten school. The president of the school kept asking what our people wanted to settle the case, but no one would answer. Finally, after the president said, "It's a quarter to three", a rookie back-bencher of ours, who was told to observe only and who was literally sitting on a piano bench, started playing the piano.

He also sang, "It's a quarter to three. There's no one in the bar. Just you and me."

The president, not thrown off his game, said, "I repeat, what do you want?"

Our rookie said, "We want your firstborn male child."

The president said, "You can't have him. I need him to support me in retirement. You can have my second born. But, at least, we are negotiating."

Thereafter, the rookie took over, and an agreement was wrapped up that afternoon. For obvious reasons no one on our team ever told me this story, but I semi-confirmed its veracity later.

*****

Since I was in the area of Higher Education, I did quite a few reviews of female versus male faculty salaries. In a way, it was like shooting moose from a helicopter. The biggest schools are in the Midwest, which was my region. I am not referring to schools like MIT, Harvard, Yale, or Stanford, but to universities that have the largest population of students, and, thus, have the largest faculty employment.

The Ohio State University, the University of Minnesota, and others had the largest single campus enrollments in the country. (As an aside, I once left the *The* out of OSU's title and my boss got an irate letter from the president of the university saying that I'd disrespected the school.) The University of Wisconsin was in the top three schools in the country for size of a multi-campus system although the reviews were by campus. Even the lesser known University of Cincinnati was the ninth largest school in the country at the time. The state of Ohio alone had eighty-six four-year colleges.

We reviewed the treatment of an employee versus the treatment of another employee. We checked for the same credentials of each employee. If, for example, being a Nobel Prize winner was required for a job, we just compared genders to see if the requirement was equally applied. If, as seen at some community colleges, the person needed an M.A. to be hired, then we checked for M.A.s. Universities were more sensitive than employers in general to the fact that our investigators were not trained (or even experts) in any or all of the fields whose employment conditions we investigated.

One incident occurred when one of my deputies told the department chair of a world class physics department (like the children of Garrison Keillor's Lake Woebegone, all departments are thought to be above average) that he didn't even take Physics in college, and had failed it in high school. While this wasn't true, Don was tired of the chair's insistence that only a world class physicist could understand his HR practices. Of course, the chair complained, and Don's smart remark cost me both time and effort to explain—it was not fun.

Another Stupid Move

Many of these stories are about other people's addle-brained actions, but this one is mine. Of course, in most cases I can explain why the dumb behavior was really okay, but in this instance, there is really no excuse for what happened. I must have taken an extra dose of "stupid" pills that morning.

My HEW office in Chicago was located in a building that had a basement that could be cut through on the way to the deli that many of us favored for the ever-healthy Italian sausage sandwich. Dividing the basement into half were two swinging doors with rubber bumpers and small plastic windows. It was designed both so that a fork lift could be driven through it and so that one could see who was coming (because the area had some daytime crime).

One day I saw three co-workers coming back from the deli, and I bent down near the doors.

When they opened the doors, I jumped up and yelled, "Arggh!" The three women whom I'd never met threw their food in the air and screamed. (Darn that opaque plastic!) As I bent down to pick up the food, I apologized, while offering the explanation, "I thought I knew you" --as if that would be a good reason to scare someone into throwing their lunch into the air.

They silently edged by me like a rat was on the floor. Nor would they let buy their lunch; they just wanted to flee the madman, which they did. For months, I didn't use the basement or that deli. I never saw those women again, either. I sometimes wonder whether they ever used the basement cut-thru or deli again.

Muhammad Ali

This may not fit perfectly into work stories, but it happened at the intersection of work and family.

My mother and father were both originally from Chicago. My mother has never been into sports, but she is into family, particularly who knows her family, and who works with her family. On her way to the airport leaving Chicago after a visit with Jackie, Michelle, and me, she gave me a call at the office. I asked about her flight and told her that she should look for Darnell White, a coworker from the Cleveland office, who was on the same flight back. Asking how she would recognize him, I described him as a light skinned African American man with freckles and a reddish-tinted Afro.

A few weeks later, Darnell came back to the Chicago office for a visit. He came in and said, "Man, you cool." While we got along, I doubted that he ever thought of me as cool.

I asked, "What did I do?"

"Well, I went to O'Hare last time I was leaving here and was waiting for my plane when I saw Muhammad Ali." (Ali lived in Chicago and was then the most recognizable athlete and, arguably, the most famous black man in the world.) "His entourage had left him for a moment so I went over and said, 'Champ, I'm a great fan.' Ali went into his public 'I am the greatest' routine which sort of disappointed me. Then along came this little old white lady.

"She came up to us and said, 'I know who you are,' and Ali puffed out his chest. The lady said, 'You're Darnell White. You work with my son Chuck.' Ali looked like his ego took an uppercut from a 115-pound woman. So I said, 'Hi. And this is Muhammad Ali.'

"Your mother held her hand out and said, 'Hello, Mr. Ali.' As far as I remember that was the whole conversation, and your mother walked away. I talked with Ali for another minute or two, and I thought he was looking at me funny."

Later I asked my mother if she remembered meeting Darnell White, and she did. I said, "Do you remember who he was with?"

"A big man in a nice suit," she said.

I must have looked incredulous that she didn't remember, so she said, "That's right. The boxer fella."

But, it's not like he worked with *her* son.

The Joy of Travel

Sometimes the excitement on a case could be the travel to and from the investigation, review, or speech. Brower Airways had the smallest planes I ever flew in, and my most memorable flight was from O'Hare to Macomb where

Western Illinois University was located. The five-passenger airplane flew at 5,000 feet over Interstate 90. The pilot loaded the luggage in the wings to balance the weight. The first passenger in sat in the co-pilot's seat and the last passenger in sat almost on the wrap-under door.

I had no desire to sit on the door on the return trip so I got in first, snagging the co-pilot's seat. The other passengers were middle-aged Canadian businessmen. The noise from the plane was very loud so only the pilot and I could hear the O'Hare tower. However, no one could hear the pilot. As we approached O'Hare, I heard, "Brower 123, this is O'Hare tower. Descend to 1,000 feet immediately."

The pilot pushed the wheel or stick straight ahead and we went straight down. The Canadians were screaming, but although I could see their mouths were open, the plane made so much noise we couldn't hear them in the cabin. I had the advantage of knowing that the pilot meant to do what he was doing. Nonetheless, I felt I'd been inserted into a World War II film of dive bombers in the Pacific. It turned out that we had missed a United Airlines flight by less than 1,000 feet, but I never saw the other plane.

*****

Sometimes when in Washington, the adventure could be on the ground. The Metro wasn't yet completed, and HEW wasn't close to any of the decent areas of the city, so we often ended up in a decent hotel in rough areas.

One of my coworkers, an African American woman, was held up on the street in broad daylight. Luckily, the teen-aged thieves just took cash. However, our coworker told us she was shocked that when she told the muggers that they didn't want to rob her because she was "a third-world woman", they just looked at her and said, "Give us the money."

A week later, I (a first-world man) had not yet gotten the message that the streets were rough. I went for a walk around eleven at night and was a few blocks from the hotel when an older car pulled over. The middle-aged African American man, dressed as if he was coming home from the second shift, rolled down his window, shook his head a little, leaned over and said, "Hey, white boy. Get your ass back in that hotel." The exact words he spoke may sound a little rough, but I think they were among the nicest, most useful I ever heard from a stranger. I went back at a trot.

A Million Dollars for a Gerund

We often got million dollar class (group) back-pay awards. This was thirty years ago when a million was a lot of money. The employers were guiltier, and more capable of shame, and we had greater power in pre-award reviews. We could do "Passovers".

The word p*assover* in this context referred to the fact that before a contract could be awarded or "let", the university had to be found compliant with EEO standards. If this could not be done in thirty days, they were *passed over* for the contract. Our findings were not judicial, much less final. Yet, we were able to block multimillion dollar contracts. Passover was declared unconstitutional a few years later when the courts ruled that schools were being denied contacts without due process.

Little government civil rights work was done at the professional or managerial employment level to start because there weren't enough women or minorities pressing into these jobs; however, the exception was universities. The women's faulty groups on campuses were the driving force and also provided expert advice. Granted, sometimes they sued to get us to do more with this issue, and even complained that what we did wasn't enough. It was a national issue. It was the golden era of EEO enforcement, and as EEOC had been the training ground in general investigations, so too was HEW as it was ahead of the curve when it came to investigations at the professional level.

This is all background to another story. We were negotiating a multimillion dollar settlement at a large university. There was a pre-award involved, and the thirty-day window was closing. In addition to this, the contract affected the co-operative launch by four nations of a satellite, which had a narrow window of opportunity and would close. If we didn't agree that the university passed EEO scrutiny, the university would be out of the project at best. At worst, the whole launch would be cancelled.

In the final negotiations, we wanted four million dollars back-pay for the women while the university had only offered three million. The final negotiations were by speakerphone. The President, University Counsel, and others were on one end of the line and my team, our counsel, a State Department lawyer (in town for cross-training purposes) and I were on the other end.

From my point of view, we were arguing about one million dollars. The President of the University, who was a former English professor, was arguing about, and was unwilling to sign, any agreement written in poor grammar.

According to him, a gerund was misplaced in one of our standard, Washington-required, paragraphs, and he wanted it corrected. I wasn't authorized to do this although I assumed he was correct.

Eventually, I caved in and told him that we would fix the gerund's grammar gaffe if he was willing to pay the extra million, and Washington be damned. When he agreed, I swear I heard his lawyer objecting across the state line through the open windows despite the phone line. The State Department lawyer found a white shirt board used by laundries, stuck a ruler through it, and silently marched around the room with a sign that said, "A million dollars for a gerund!"

Yes, Washington complained. They 'let' the case go through, flawed as it was by the gerund being changed from its required spot. Further, those in Washington let me know that, as in all things, they could have done a better job. I can't resist being snarky enough to add that they never had and never did.

The Twins

Rarely the incentive to settle was not just about avoiding negative publicity or damning evidence. A case I considered to be amusing was part of a larger review, but involved my being able to interview nineteen-year-old twins—one female, the other male. They had graduated from the same high school with the same GPA having taken the same courses. They were hired the same day for the same position of lab tech. He was paid seventy-five cents more per hour than she. While there were eight other women and fourteen other men in this same situation, these were the only twins hired with the exact same qualifications and background.

The administrator in charge of the university's medical school didn't want to settle. For such a simple case, I didn't feel like flying several hundred miles back to the office, writing the case up, issuing a finding, and then fighting the case for months.

The job itself was 100% paid by a federal grant. I don't remember how we got hold of the conditions of the grant, but we did. Lo and behold, the grant stipulated that all lab techs were to be paid at the higher rate ($ .75 more an hour) even though the med school wasn't paying the women that rate.

We went into a meeting with both the medical school director and the university counsel. I showed them the paperwork. I further told them that I didn't investigate grant fraud and knew how life was. I said I figured that they probably used the extra money to purchase microscopes that some silly grant rule didn't cover. Nonetheless, since the grantor was HEW and that I worked for HEW, I would have to tell the granting agency that some of the lab techs weren't being paid as the school claimed they were. That is, *unless* the women got back-pay, interest, and pay raises before I left the campus. The counsel agreed at once while the medical school director fumed and was ignored.

*****

While I said (above) that I didn't know how we got hold of the grant information, that part is true. It is likely, however, that we got it from the clerical staff. Clerical staffs generally knew what was going on, but they seemed invisible to the company or school managers. It was not unusual to get information easily from clerical staffs, especially in group gender discrimination cases. Moreover, I don't recall a case in which the management ever openly suspected the clerical staff's involvement.

One incident in which the clerical staff leaked us memos involved the case of the trainee who had sat on the piano bench. The representatives of ten major universities located in my region got together and then went to Washington to complain about our aggressive investigations. They had held a meeting beforehand to plan what they would say. The meeting also covered our probable tactics during negotiations. Thanks to our source, we reviewed their minutes shortly after they were written. I especially enjoyed reading about our use of the "silent man" gambit as a psychological means to throw them off.

It was this same trainee who had started to sing, "it's a quarter to three" during a negotiation that had also sat in on other negotiations with these same universities whose representatives traveled to Washington. Since he was a trainee during these negotiations, he was introduced and then proceeded to sit in the second row and observe the events. What we hadn't known was the universities wanted to know the *real* reason he was silent, and further that his presence there had unnerved them.

Sometimes the games get way too complicated. In this case, our "silent man" was silent because he was a trainee who was told to observe and learn from the process. We had enough to do in negotiations without expending the energy or playing too many tactical games. Besides, as I often told trainees, telling the truth is a great tactic. The truth is easy to remember, and it confuses the lawyers.

HEW Legal Support

At most agencies the lawyers come from the Office of the General Counsel. At the HEW office in D.C., the person who answered the phone always greeted me with an officious, "This is General Counsel. Who are you and what is your business?"

I told her that I was General Foods calling about a cereal case, and she put me through to the lawyer I was seeking.

Thereafter, I called as General Motors about a car case, and as General Confusion about mental health cases. She never flinched and always put me through. I know that I used this ploy at least three times before an attorney told me, "Stop doing that! It's not funny. She doesn't get it!"

In spite of their generally weak enforcement efforts, all Washington government attorneys are more committed than you—whoever you are. Remember, as I said…they *are* more learned just by being from Washington.

Disclaimer: Two of the best lawyers, one in Chicago, the other in Washington, I ever worked with were from HEW.

DOL

When I moved back to Cleveland, a consolidated office of several civil rights agencies was opened. People from the DOD, HEW, GSA, etc. were combined into one office under the Department of Labor called the Office of Federal Contracts Compliance Programs (OFCCP). We had plenty of space, but very little furniture. We were located in a private building in Lakewood, but the government General Services Administration (GSA) leased several floors of this building. We occupied all but one corner of one floor. I asked the GSA rep what was in the corner section that no one ever visited. He told me it contained excess furniture. Since we needed furniture, I asked to see it.

It was great! There was two offices' worth—fit for a CEO and an administrative assistant. I wasn't used to such good stuff, but since it was free, and the inventory just listed the pieces as *desk, chair*, etc., I swept everything up. The glass top of the executive desk required two men to carry it across the hall. "How had this furniture been allowed to sit without a claimant?" I asked.

I was told that no one from in-town would touch it because it was tainted. The previous "owner" had been caught paying rent for a girlfriend's apartment and, further, had furnished the Gold Coast digs with expensive furnishings paid for by his agency. He had been sent to jail. For many months no one wanted *his* office furniture. No one, that is, until I came along from out of town.

A few months later I received a call from the Executive Assistant to the Secretary's Representative for the Midwest Region. They had heard that I had executive furniture. Because the Secretary's Rep had furniture that wasn't quite as good as mine, and she outranked me, she was confiscating mine. I agreed, said it was fine, but that I wouldn't release the furniture until replacements arrived.

After a few weeks, the pieces arrived, were fairly nice, so I released my executive furniture. Actually, there was little suffering on my part. In fact, I had been taking ribbing over the size of the furniture. I had been told that I looked like a peanut behind the desk, and further, that I looked like I was sitting in a hole, trying to look over the desk.

Two weeks later, I happened to be in Chicago so I decided to go over to the Secretary's Rep's office to introduce myself as well as "visit" my furniture. It hadn't arrived yet, and because they had already shipped their furniture to me, they had no furniture at all. The phones were on the floor, and the Rep was using a card table and folding chair in the meantime. I think that the furniture arrived, albeit scratched, several weeks later.

At the same time we received furniture, we also managed to dig up quite a few room dividers which lessened the bowling alley feel of the office. Later on, the staff moved into cubicles, which are not soundproof by the way. Etiquette demands, therefore, dulcet tones on the phone. Unfortunately, one of our investigators was more suited to being a pirate with a knife in his teeth yelling "Aargh!" at the top of his lungs. While we tried not to listen to his arguments with his wife, one day everyone ended up laughing as he boomed out, "I don't care...Then, you tell Timmy to bite the dog!"

The B.S. Detector Comes Back

I inherited several former co-workers including my buddies from the days of the old automatic B.S. detector in the new, consolidated EEO office. As soon as I started holding staff meetings, I occasionally saw one or the other hold the detector just above the table level signaling the other. Not as funny, I thought.

To compound matters, they had added to the routine. Apparently, I'd say, "That's the law," Or "That's the regulation" during meetings, and according to them, quite often. When the meeting would break for lunch, they would exit quoting from the old movie, *Island of Lost Souls* or its remake, *Island of Dr. Moreau*. For those unfamiliar with the movie, Dr. Moreau was a mad scientist who tried to clone humans and animals and was only partially successful. His (partial) successes lived in caves on his island. Eventually they revolted.

Behind my back, I'd hear, "What *is* the law?" and the feeble attempt to mimic the sound of a whip cracking.

The response: "Not to walk on all fours."

Again, "What *is* the law?" followed again by the whip cracking.

Finally, "Not to eat the flesh of man."

Once they'd put me in my place, we'd go eat lunch.

Administration DOL-style

When carbon copies were still utilized, we had different color carbons for the original, the case file, the back-up file, and supervisor's file, etc. When colored carbons were no longer available, we photocopied everything. Forgetting that the color had meaning, the clerical staff wrote on each page "green" copy, "red" copy, "blue" copy instead of filing the non-original copies in the appropriate place. This wasn't the stupidity of the locals; it was a regional rule.

*****

When we first got personal computers and software, it took a couple years for our region to stop insisting that we hand enter case file data, mail it to Chicago where it would be entered into *the* computer, rather than *a* computer, send

86

it to D.C., and then show up electronically back at our office. When I suggested that we enter the data in Cleveland, and get reviewed online in Chicago to save steps, you would have thought that I was trying to lead a revolution.

*****

Time off for good behavior is not just for prison inmates. At DOL we had "Good Job" awards. The government can provide only limited financial incentives for exemplary performance. Certainly, there is no profit sharing, either. Thus, a decision was made that if a person was very productive or exemplary at work (and if one was the type we wished to encourage to continue this practice of good work), on rare occasions, we would send a person home to do *no* work for a day with pay (a paid-day off). That is the reason why the "Good Job" award was nicknamed "Time Off for Good Behavior."

On the flip side, however, I had a deputy, replying to anyone who complained of limited facilities or training, who would say in a deadpan voice, "Nothing…is too good for our people" or "If there wasn't a better way, we wouldn't do it this way."

Some DOL Cases

This incident occurred during the latter part of my career when I was on a project in hi-tech Silicon Valley. At one of the companies we found that forty software designers and programmers had identified themselves as American Indians. I asked the HR VP what was going on since we both knew that there were fewer than ten Native American software design engineers in the whole country. He checked and came back with the explanation that these were their Asian Indian (green card) design engineers who knew nothing about American EEO issues. All had checked the box "American Indian" as opposed to "Asian Indian" just to show how (Rah! Rah! America!) patriotic towards the United States they were.

*****

Speaking of other foreign issues, sometimes the owners of a company were foreign, and the employees were (local) citizens. I was sent in to conciliate an issue at a company in which one of our teams had run into a situation regarding gender discrimination. The company had hired only male forklift operators and refused to hire women for this job. It was 1990, and thus, a no-brainer.

The president of the division had been sent by his father-in-law, the CEO, from France to shake the company up, and he had. I was told that the son-in-law walked around with an aide who carried a clipboard. The Division President (the son-in-law) asked all the non-union people what their title was, what they did, and how many of "you" (people with the same title) there were. Then, reportedly, he'd often turn to his aide and said something to the effect, "Twelve is too many. Fire seven!" He wasn't popular and didn't care.

Sure, I will admit that his English was better than my French; however, his accent was straight Inspector Clouseau of Pink Panther fame, and this just added to what the locals thought of him. During the early part of the meeting, he turned to me and stated rather imperiously, "You must understand. Ziss can not be. In France we do not haav women drive ze forkleeft."

I said, "That is great. The problem is solved."

"How so?" he asked me.

"This isn't France. I am glad to learn about French labor practices, but here women drive forklifts. You own the company, but have U.S. federal contracts. You signed a contract to follow U.S. EEO law. End of discussion."

Okay, we won the case, but that isn't the point. That came later. The discussion was over so quickly that we ended up going out to lunch with the company lawyer, the EEO director, and a couple other HR-types. As soon as we reached the parking lot, they literally (not figuratively) started slapping me on the back, high-fiving, and saying, "All right!" They had all told the president exactly what I'd told him and had been treated to his *hauteur*. They loved seeing someone whom the boss could not fire tell him off and get away with it.

*****

Sometimes companies hurt themselves through their actions. One such company had an EEO/HR director who happened to be part Native American. He felt he could tell by looking if a person was partially or completely of Native American heritage despite the fact that the person may or may not have identified him or herself that way. When he recorded applicants for entry level jobs, he ended up with nearly 15% Native American applicants in a 2% Native American workforce area. When recording ethnic background of hires, he compounded the problem by letting the person's self-identification stand. This meant that the company sent in a report to the government that said they had a 15% Native American applicant flow rate for entry level jobs, but only hired Native Americans at a 2% rate.

Nothing gets the federal government's EEO apparatus as excited as when it is told that the hiring of a particular minority group is at a rate significantly below their application rate, especially when the company is silent about relative qualifications. Now, there is scrutiny! When it is explained how the problem was a recording error, the first reaction of the investigators is *Cover up!* In a sense, the company has blown the whistle on itself. When the error is compounded with the explanation that it was caused by an internal over-riding of a significant number of the applicants' self-identification, then the company is very lucky if it gets away with spending only tens of thousands of dollars on the re-view. If it is found that discrimination didn't actually occur, there is still an agreement made to "play nice from now on" and to send in reports that would not have been necessary had the original error not been made.

Gary's Cases

Gary is one of those nutty (mostly in a good way) gov-ernment employees; I worked with him at both DOD and DOL. The first time I went out with Gary on a review should have tipped me off to the fact that not everything he did or said would be bland or government-grey. On the way to a defense plant's co-review of a steel plant, he needed to stop on the way out of town to pick something up at his mother's house. While we were there, Gary said something which elicited a response that she muttered under her breath. While it seemed like only three or four words, I couldn't understand it and asked Gary what she had said.

He said, "It is Yiddish and doesn't translate well."

I said, "It was only a few words. Try."

"Well," Gary said, "It's roughly: if a dog had your thoughts, in his head, he'd go crazy." Apparently, a lot can be packed into three or four words of Yiddish.

Typical of the times, the steel plant, that Gary and I vis-ited, wasn't hiring women. I was trying to negotiate a hiring plan that was well under the percentage of women in the workforce when the HR chief asked if I was serious. "Hell no," Gary piped up. "Just hire one or two and let them in-jure their backs and he'll be satisfied."

In spite of this, throughout his career Gary handled some very good cases. All were old-fashioned—that is, he hated statistics. If he had a class (group) case, he figured out the harm to each individual before making a finding as if he were investigating as many cases as there were victims.

This led to a case at DOL in which he had fifteen black assistant store manager promotion applicants who, we felt, were denied jobs because of race. Some of the cases were stronger than others and, before the opening of negotiations, we decided that Gary would present the cases one at a time with the strongest case first.

The company team was led by a very dignified, older Senior VP of Human Resources. However, lower level managers were also there to present rebuttal to whatever we said. Gary started with his first case and showed how the black internal promotion applicant was more qualified than the two whites promoted to this position.

In rebuttal, the company representative responded by saying that while what Gary had said was true, Gary had missed the negative interview notes on the back of the black applicant's file. Then he proceeded to show Gary the back side of the file where the notes were.

Gary's response: "That's why I copied the back side of the file." At this, he showed his copy of the blank back to the Senior VP, and then said that when he had been at the company nine months after this person's interview, he had made sure to copy both sides of the file. At that time, although these notes were supposedly written at the time of the interview, they weren't in the file.

The Senior VP stood, looked at his people, and bellowed, "Who did this to ME!"

Apparently he didn't like being embarrassed. We never had to present our weaker cases; the company settled right away, and someone lost his job. None of this would have happened had Gary not copied blank files. As far as I know, he was the only person who copied blank files.

In another of his cases, for which Gary never forgave me, I turned down his recommended finding for a Viet Nam veteran. The unchallenged facts were that the complainant was an automatic weapon-carrying probationary guard at a nuclear power plant. In front of both management and union officials, he made several inflammatory statements including that, as a Viet Nam vet, he was likely, at any moment, to go off and spray the other employees with lead or shoot up the nuclear containment vessel. For this, he was fired.

Gary wanted the company found guilty because they had not obtained a psychiatrist's opinion as to the likelihood that the man was serious.

The general principle in a risky employee situation is this: the bigger the risk, the lower the rebuttal is needed by the company to carry the day. In this case, I told Gary I was issuing a "not guilty" finding. He was irate. What possible reason could I have to find the company not guilty? I told him the bottom line was that I lived downwind of the plant.

He also had a smoking allergy case in which the company doctor claimed that the employee wasn't allergic to smoke although her own physician claimed that she was. For this case, we got a third, tie-breaker opinion, paid for by the government. Gary attended the exam. When he returned, I asked, "What did the doctor do?"

He said, "The doctor put the complainant in an all-glass, sealed room, and then pumped smoke in to see if she coughed." She did. So much for a third opinion.

*****

Gary kept a 3X5 card with words that he had heard mispronounced by several of his minority co-workers. When a minority secretary pronounced the word *ask* as "ax", he'd go into a chopping motion. That is, until one day the secretary said, "What are you, a grammararatarian?"

Sexual harassment eventually became recognized as illegal. Never missing a chance to state a half-truth and be a throwback, Gary learned that asking a coworker out on a date is not harassment as long as the person wasn't his/her boss and as long as, when told to back off, the action isn't repeated. Now, there are many other acts that are considered harassment the first time they occur. Gary ignored that fact. He walked around his super sensitive female coworkers saying, "Remember, the first time is free." He felt that any minority or woman who complained about him was just too touchy.

March Madness

Like most workforces we became more sensitive to smaller and smaller issues as time went on. Also like others, our early handling of such issues was clunky. One such example was the NCAA March Madness basketball pool. The pools aren't random, but are tests of ability to predict winners over several elimination rounds for sixty-five teams. For decades, women have not only participated, but won. In fact, my daughter won her pool several years ago.

Twenty-five years ago we decided that it wasn't fair that most women did not want to participate. If it was our intention that all women join the pool, whether or not they cared about the basketball tournaments, then we needed a way to make the pool fair to all. The only "fair" system was a blind draw of teams. This made the pool fair since it was a lottery, but defeated its purpose to test the skill and provide bragging rights to the winner. Under this "fair" system, no one would be advantaged by having followed the college basketball season.

The year our sensitivity kicked in on the basketball pool happened to be the last year that U.C.L.A. was a prohibitive favorite. The first person to draw her team's name happened to be the woman with the least amount of interest in sports of any kind. She reached in, pulled out her slip, and read it.

"Ew. I have Ucklah. What is that and is it good?"

The few basketball fans just groaned and walked away. We didn't have a basketball pool after that.

Labor Lawyers: Ours

Regarding federal lawyers, some were great. Some were awful. Many of the better ones left. They had the same in-house joke we had, which was: This job is an IQ test. The longer you stay, the more stupid you are. I stayed over thirty years. One excellent lawyer, Don, who left, told me: "I loved what my job was supposed to be." I knew exactly what he meant. On the other hand, I need to add that I know of at least two very good lawyers who are still at DOL.

Don also told me that when he was thrown into his first big case, alone and untrained, against four partners and a large support staff at a mega-law firm, he just hoped they wouldn't hurt him. His own boss, the Assistant Regional Solicitor, told him that the Executive Order (No. 11246) he was enforcing was unconstitutional. Nice to know that you've got my back.

Labor Department attorneys, at least the ones outside of Washington, tend to work on more than one type of case. Don really hated Black Lung disability cases. Our lawyers represented the government against people claiming Black Lung disability. Often, the victims had no attorney to represent them. He had one case in southeast Ohio where the lawyer-less victim was called to a hearing to determine why he shouldn't be denied benefits as a result of his not coming to the last hearing.

"I couldn't come, Judge," said the man.

"Why not?" said the Administrative Law Judge.

"I was in the hospital," said the man.

"With what?" said the ALJ.

"Black Lung," said the victim, picking that moment to cough black gunk into his white hanky.

Don said he was happy to lose that case.

*****

At the Department of Labor, the attorneys come from the Solicitor of Labor (SOL). Cleveland has a rare substation called the Associate Regional Solicitor of Labor (AR-SOL).

Locally, we said that if it was necessary to go to the Solicitor, you were SOL meaning S*** out of luck, especially if serviced by the ARSOL (sound it out with a cockney accent for elucidation if necessary).

We called our negotiations *conciliation meetings*. In my mind, this was a negotiating tool itself. *Conciliation* assumes there has been a problem, and the only way to bring the company into compliance with the law is to conciliate. There is no consideration as to *whether* the law was violated, only consideration as to how to fix the problem.

Luckily, I liked negotiation because the SOL could afford to send lawyers only to very few negotiations. This meant that most negotiations were conducted by (government) non-lawyers against lawyers in order to fashion a legal document. The SOL protected the process by requiring that two pages of "General Provisions" be inserted into every agreement. Lawyers for the other side argued that some of the provisions made no sense or that the provisions should be negotiated, but we were told that the General Provisions were the Sanctum Sanctorum (the Holy of Holies) of conciliation agreements.

When the earliest grammar checking software programs were introduced, we had one that circulated for our use in

95

all documents. I inserted the generic General Provisions. Luckily, we were past the use of vacuum tubes in computers, or we would have seen smoke coming from the CPU. If the program had been a video pinball game, we would have heard "ding, ding, ding," and the screen would have shown only *TILT*. Over half of the general provisions were underlined, highlighted, crossed out, or found to be nonsensical.

Wherever I worked, our attorneys always wanted only our *best* cases. This was understandable; it was also unrealistic. With some exceptions, we settled our best cases without going into enforcement mode because the other side realized it had a loser. As it was, whenever we did settle, the other side claimed they would have beaten us at trial, but that they had settled to spare the client the costs of litigation. Sometimes, publicity was among the costs of litigation.

We also settled our worst cases by backing off because we knew they were losers. It was only the case that had 65-35 or better odds in our favor that we brought forward. The other side was calling our bluff, sometimes successfully; or they felt they had some issue of law or principle on their side. Most of the time, when we took a slam-dunk forward, the other side settled at the pretrial stage.

Internal politics often plays a role in settling cases. Lawyers play "give me the credit" like anyone else. While not leading, I was involved in a large (over ten million dollars) female back-pay discrimination case that was being settled against a national company with sites and divisions in several states. SOL Washington was sending a national office representative, despite the fact that we already had a local DOL attorney in the room, to approve the final details. The Washington lawyer arrived so late that all we had left was the wording of how we weren't covering the issue of race on this particular case; however, this didn't exonerate the company of its race issues.

From the start, the SOL rep from the national office disagreed with the proposal even *before* she read it. The corporate counsel realized well before the rest of us that the Washington SOL representative had been sent solely to block a settlement on any terms. After a couple attempts to settle, this savvy corporate counsel made an offer that I have never before nor after ever heard a lawyer make. She offered to let the SOL draft any language on the topic and pledged (in advance) that the company would agree to whatever language Washington wanted. Our Washington lawyer said, "No." Although unspoken, it was clear that the Solicitor of Labor wanted the settlement stopped so it could sent to Washington where it would be held up for some months, and then closed, thus crediting the SOL.

Who cares about the victims? The case was held up, the company extracted millions of dollars in concessions a few months later, but the headquarters' SOL got its "credit". That is, except for those few who knew what had happened!

*****

Another case that involved our Washington lawyers was a case that was first investigated by Bill, an excellent investigator at our agency. Bill was investigating a chemical plant in which some of the compounds were considered to be Placenta Carcinogenic. Placenta carcinogenic means that women of childbearing capability who have been exposed run the risk of passing cancer onto any fetus they may be carrying. The company claimed that protective gear would not prevent the problem and thus forbade women of childbearing potential from working in those areas. Further, they also allowed women to skip the area in a pay raise line of progression and to allow promotions without passing through the job in question.

At this time, the government had one of the 'liner-in, liner-out' situations. By OSHA standards, it was forbidden to let women do this job, yet by our agency, it was forbidden to keep them out of this job. Bill refused to find against the company and asked for a legal opinion. I agreed with his assessment, and the case was sent to Washington. Our national SOL quickly decided that we were idiots who didn't know that the company was clearly guilty. Further, they "knew" no harm would come to women.

Nonetheless, they deigned to come and meet with us, as well as the company representatives at the site in question. The corporate physician showed up and explained the situation. He even provided evidence for our Washington lawyers that the protective gear lessened the exposure, and while limited exposure was okay, that long-term exposure of an employee caused a heightened risk of cancer in fetuses. The federal attorneys pooh-poohed everything he said.

Then it was time to tour the facility to see the jobs and the areas in question. One of our attorneys was a woman approximately thirty years of age. Despite the apparent (total) safeness, she refused to walk through the area. The attorneys left with the file, the company officials laughed, and we never heard of a resolution of the case.

Eventually, the Supreme Court settled the issue. We returned to reviewing the chemical plant, allowing the same system to remain in place as when Bill first stepped foot inside the plant.

Labor Lawyers: Theirs

One outside counsel sent word to me that he felt that I was avoiding him whenever he appeared as counsel. Moreover, he indicated that I made little effort before sending his cases to enforcement. For the most part he represented large companies, especially utilities. Several of these companies had a shared legal policy of not settling cases (meritorious or not) without enforcement because they didn't want to be perceived as having "deep pockets". They wanted future claimants to know that they'd have to go through hell to win and that there was no cheap money to be had.

I saw this lawyer in the hallway at a conference. I told him that I thought he was a fine fellow, but that he was right. I was avoiding spending time on conciliation when he was involved, and he asked me why. I told him that we had come to realize that his appearance on behalf of a client meant three things:

1) the victims were African American
2) the client was guilty
3) and, he was under orders not to settle.

At this, he sort of half-smiled, and said, "Hmmm." I think that was the last time he was on one of my cases.

*****

Once we ran into a lawyer who just couldn't take the silliness of her client's position. It was either that or she just couldn't resist a zinger at her client's expense. Our lawyer, Bill, and I (from Department of Labor's OFCCP) were in a conciliation meeting with three lawyers, the HR VP, and the EEO Director. Among the many issues we found requiring back-pay was the refusal to hire or promote qualified women into "heavy" jobs and the failure to promote more senior minority blue-collar workers per the union contract.

At this point in time these two issues had been resolved ten years earlier; in other words, they were legally dead and solidly on our side. Not only that, but two of the company lawyers were formerly Regional Counsel for EEOC and knew the law.

First, these two made the ridiculous argument that minorities clustered themselves in lower paid jobs on purpose because they could "talk stuff." They ignored the fact that these minorities generally had greater seniority than the whites and could "talk stuff" at higher pay if they used their seniority to get promoted.

Then these men turned to the issue of the "heavy" jobs. Their arguments: women couldn't lift; they might hurt their backs; they just wanted the jobs so that they could get workers' compensation. The third lawyer, a woman who served as outside counsel, just gaped at her seniors as they made these arguments. Things got heated, and one of the male lawyers suggested a bathroom break. To which she said, "Sounds like a good idea. At least there won't be any heavy lifting there." Our team thought the remark was hilarious.

When we re-assembled after the break, the young woman wasn't with her team, and nothing was ever said. Since she'd flown in from New York with a senior partner, we never knew if she waited in a car, or returned alone, with or without her job.

*****

I had a case near the end of my career in which the in-house counsel wanted to settle the case quickly. There were several issues in this case including one for back-pay and jobs for minority clericals not hired because of race. I wanted up to eighteen months of back-pay, the most allowed under the circumstances. Rightfully, he wanted a reduction for diligent search for work, which means that if someone is denied a job wrongfully, they must continue to search for work elsewhere. When work is found, assuming the position pays as much as the job denied, back-pay ceases to accumulate. So, he proposed six months maximum back-pay, and we came to an impasse.

At the time it was a hot job market, and these were entry-level jobs. The company lawyer told me he really wanted to settle the case. He asked, "Why don't you call the Ohio Bureau of Employment Services (OBES) and find out how long a diligent search for work would have taken these victims?"

I called the relevant OBES expert, explained the situation, and said, "How long would it have taken for these folks to find work after they were turned down?"

He said, "Well, that depends."

I asked, "Depends on what?"

"On how late in the day they were turned down," he answered.

I presume the lawyer had called the unemployment office before I did. I grabbed the six months' back-pay offer he had left open and was very grateful. Per usual, my regional and national office told me they could have gotten more back-pay. They dithered for the next six months while the money deflated, and the victims became harder to locate. Then they settled.

*****

My admin assistant accused me of "only favoring Bill because he is competent." Uh huh; that may have not been the only reason, but it was a good one.

This same person, now working for Bill who reported to me, filed a race complaint and lost, then followed with a sex complaint and also lost. One day I was on the phone with the regional EEO officer who took all the complaints. He was retiring, and I had called to say good-bye. From there, our conversation moved to the following:

He started by saying, "I'm not supposed to discuss this, but, what the heck, Chuck, I'm retiring."

"Discuss what?" I asked.

"Well, Ms.(Jones) called a while back. She wanted to file a religious discrimination charge. I asked if Duffy or Bill knew her religion. She told me no. Given her two earlier baseless charges I just told her I'm not taking the charge even though I had no authority to refuse it."

Since we were breaking rules, I broke one, too. I said, "I don't know her religion, but what is it?"

He told me her religion. It turns out that she, her supervisor, and I all share the same religion.

Some of the "Crazies" are in Supervision

There were plenty of seemingly crazy government employees at DOL. Not all of them were non-supervisory. One of the better moments with one of my first DOL bosses happened one morning. Per usual, he called me with the greeting, "This is Ray" which always sounded like "sssss Raaaaay." He continued with, "What's new?"

I told him, "Same old, same old."

He said, "I want you to show cause Ford." (This means find them guilty.)

"There's several (facilities) in the district. Which one?"

"I don't care. Pick one."

At this point the conversation was already beyond weird, but I pushed forward.

"On what grounds?"

"Race," he said.

Race is a basis upon which someone can charge another person, but it is not grounds or the reason to find them guilty. I said, "I can't do that, Ray. I don't even have a Ford case open."

"Open one. They discriminated against my uncle in St. Louis," he said, clearly impatient. At that time our region did not cover St. Louis so Ray could not order anyone in St. Louis to "get" Ford.

"I can't do that, Ray," I said.

He yelled, "Shut your fucking mouth!" His deputy later told me he was still talking when I slammed the phone down.

A minute later, the phone rang. "SSSSS Raaaay. I hope you didn't just hang up on me."

I said, "I didn't hang up on you any more than you told me to shut my fucking mouth."

He said, "Well, I hope you didn't hang up on me."

I repeated my lines. He repeated his. I think this went on ten or fifteen times before the call ended.

Jim, his deputy, said Ray then turned to him and said, "Jim, I think I made him mad."

I never heard about show causing Ford again.

Ray was so off the wall that sometimes I played crazy-dumb with him. Once, when he accused me of being in a cabal with two other district directors, I creatively missed the point and told him that was impossible.

"Why?" he asked.

"Because CABAL is an acronym made up of the first letter of the last names of five conspirators who tried to overthrow the Third French Republic. You need five for a cabal," I said.

He just clenched his jaw, hissed at me, and then turned and went to lunch. I never heard about a conspiracy again, must less a cabal.

*****

Ray seemed crazy, but sometimes the people he went after were crazy, too. Len was a colleague who also happened to be my friend whom Ray fired on trumped-up charges. At the trial, the judge found out that Len was fired because all the cases that his office completed the previous two years were rejected. He also found out that all the cases had been approved until the day Ray decided to fire Len. Up until that day, all of Len's cases that had already been "quality audited" were now recalled, sent to Ray, and then instantly rejected. Because Len's office had not done a single quality case in two years, Len had to be fired.

One EEO officer recounted three colleagues talking about Len when Ray said, "What's a fifty-year-old white Jew doing in the program anyways?"

Len responded, "I'm not Jewish."

Ray also proudly recounted another reason that Len was fired. He told the judge that Len had failed to pony up the required contribution for a present for the Agency head, who was leaving because of the Reagan election. Ray was very proud that all but two of his managers had contributed to this fund. (I was the other one, by the way.) He continued with the fact that among the Regional Directors, he had given the Agency Director the best gift. In his decision, the judge mentioned that he was surprised that Ray bragged about a crime. For it is a crime to *require* employees to contribute money for a present to a superior.

When Len won the case, he had to be reinstated. It happened to be December 7th when Ray's boss called a pre-Rodney King "Can't we all just get along" meeting. Len proudly told me what happened during this meeting. Ray, the government's lawyer, Will Hashimoto, the boss's assistant, Len and his attorney all attended. The boss suggested that they all shake hands, but Len declined to shake Hashimoto's hand. He said, "I never shake hands with Japanese on December seventh." He thought what he said was hilarious. To make matters worse, Will had never turned on Len, and frankly, Hashimoto had been born in an internment camp during World War II.

There was even more to the story about the present than was presented at the trial. Len, another manager, and I were in a bar in San Antonio the night before the last conference held during the Carter administration when that White House-appointed Agency Director came over. He asked, "Len, how's it going?"

Len said, "Fine, since the election." (The election of Reagan meant that the Director would lose his job.)

This remark caused the two of them to go at each other. The other manager and I stepped between them. He took one punch to the chest, and I, being shorter, took a hit to the cheek before we broke them up. Between the two of them, they *decided* that since they hadn't hit each other, and both were in the wrong, that nothing needed to be done.

*****

I suppose, in retrospect, that this is better than what I heard happened in management after I retired. At a conference all District Directors were asked by their new boss if they'd meet their production goals for the quarter. Some said yes, but others said that not only that would they meet their goals, but they would exceed their goals by a certain percentage. Those that indicated that they'd only just meet their goals were deemed "disloyal" and had to sit facing the wall, not taking notes for the rest of the day while their deputies sat at the conference table in their place.

I would never have sat facing the wall. One District Director retired a few months later; his wife told me that he retired a few years earlier than he planned. Another had a heart attack shortly thereafter and then retired. These two were leading, experienced people, who, by the way, met the goals while most of those who promised to exceed their goals never did.

*****

I'm part of an informal group of former District Directors who have gotten together a few times. At our first meeting, we assembled on a cool evening around a grill on a deck in suburban Chicago. The newest retiree asked the group, "When do the nightmares stop?" As if it were the most normal question in the world, we mulled it over and came up with the consensus of around two years.

Some Crazies Weren't in Supervision...Some Used to Be

Nothing undercuts a manager more than crazy performance by investigators in the field. Each story gets re-told ad infinitum throughout business and *just shows* how government employees are (fill in the blank with the appropriate negative). The job of stopping discrimination is also undercut by this. Worse, some employees treated their jobs as being for their psychic benefit. They would return to the office claiming they'd sure told that company off. Further, it was too bad that management was too chicken to support their great work.

Of course, if all they had done was tell the company off, and, if they failed to gather evidence, management couldn't support them. As a result, if women or minorities had been shafted, they stayed shafted.

*****

Referencing back to the guy who showed off his beat-up car, he ended up working for me at the Department of Labor. While I have changed the names of most characters in these stories, he will remain nameless. At one time he had been the District Director in another city, but was downgraded and sent to our office.

This event didn't cause him to be downgraded, but nonetheless, it was a classic. When he first took over his DOL district office, it was located on an Army base near a large Midwestern city. He came in with several others when several agencies were consolidated into one. Like me, he ran into the same situation of having plenty of space, but little furniture. The Army base was DOD, but he was just a DOL tenant of the DOD; thus DOD couldn't help out on his obtaining furniture for his office.

Quite early on in his tenure, he told his two deputies to meet him Sunday at a certain base gate at a given time. When the deputies arrived, they met their new director dressed in his outdated Major's uniform, standing next to a large Army truck. He threw one of them the keys and said, "Here. Majors don't drive." The three of them proceeded to the supply area where the excess furniture was stored. After loading up chairs, desks, and file cabinets, they drove through various gates, using the director's name and rank, to their offices. At which point, they unloaded the furniture and then returned the truck.

On Monday morning the base commander, a colonel, phoned, apparently livid. "How dare you impersonate an officer and steal furniture!" the colonel raged, wanting to know.

The man ("our hero") responded by telling the colonel that the uniform he'd worn was his own, that he'd never said he was on active duty, and that the furniture wasn't stolen. Further, it was still on the base in the Director's offices, out in the open. Finally, he told the colonel that he expected to be thanked for creating valuable space in the excess furniture building. The colonel sputtered a bit, got off the phone, but never did anything else in regards to the furniture. We all assumed he saw the twisted logic behind the furniture move.

Not all of his schemes were harmless, however. One time he ate all the free donuts a company's HR department put out for both visitors and staff. This former Director also had diabetes, and this stunt caused him to have a "sugar swoon". He had to be picked up by two members of our staff: one to drive him, and another to pick up the government car.

Ultimately, though, he ended up retiring to prevent his being fired. After many other problems such as lying, cheat-

107

ing, and in one case, threatening to find a company out of compliance if they didn't provide him a job reference, he reached the end of the line. He already was at a warning status, but in this last event, he drove a government-issued car one hundred miles from the office. During this trip up and back, he managed to put seven hundred and fifty miles on the odometer. He also charged three breakfasts on his per diem for the day as well.

I asked him to explain the breakfasts, and he did. First, the former Director said he went to breakfast near the hotel. While driving to the company under review, he saw a diner from his youth. He explained that he had grown up in the city where the review was taking place, and he felt compelled to go in and eat there.

This second breakfast made him late getting to the company. The HR Director was upset and said, "I skipped breakfast to be on time for you, and you don't even show up until 10:30?"

"So," said my soon-to-be ex-employee, "I had to take the guy out to breakfast and pay for it."

His own union rep, who was in the room as the three-breakfast man explained the situation, just shook his head.

*****

I also inherited an employee who had been part of an *upward mobility* program for clericals. Many people in these upward mobility programs worked out fine as investigators, but occasionally one took the job just to get paid more with no real intention of going out in the field and confronting employers. This employee froze up during an on-site review. The HR Director phoned and said, "Your person here is frozen and not talking." Of course, managers of federal investigators are used to HR people or company lawyers calling to get around an investigator. This Director had even skipped the woman's supervisor in his phone call to me.

So, I wasn't too receptive to this call and made a dismissive remark. The HR person said, "No, really. She's frozen. Do you want to talk to her?"

I said, "Yes," but when they gave her the phone, she didn't talk. I said, "Mary, are you afraid?"

She said, "Yes," but it sounded like "Y-y-y-e-s-s-s." I asked if she wanted to come back to the office and got the same answer. I asked if someone needed to get her. Same answer.

*****

One of our better investigators got off to a rocky start. I asked him why he checked *force* in the application question: Do you favor the overthrow of the government by force or violence? He answered that he thought it was a weird either/or question, but that *force* sounded better than *violence*.

*****

By the time I was about ready to leave government work, my agency's standards had apparently sunk very low in regards to hiring quality individuals. In our conference room, a lady was interviewing for a job as a mid-level investigator. She had a master's degree in social science and some experience at a sister agency. At the end of the interview she was asked (as is normal), "Do you have any questions for us?"

She said, "Well, yes, I have one. Can you guarantee that I won't be sent into the field at places where I can't find a hotel that will take my parrot? I take him on trips and, while I don't expect to take him on-site to a company, he has to be able to stay at my hotel."

How would you like to be the maid coming into a room with a talking parrot, especially if not briefed beforehand? By the way, she was offered the job, but turned *us* down.

*****

Because we didn't receive many applications from those who worked in private industry with a HR background, there were few hires among them. When we finally hired someone from industry, he insisted that he just needed to study the law because he knew all about how industry works and how to get along with people. On his first case, he asked to see the president, in-house counsel, and the HR director. They all came to the conference room, and then he slapped a list on the table and said, "All right, you birds, here's the shit I need!" Not surprisingly, that review didn't go well.

*****

I am not the only EEO vet with weird employee stories; I heard many from other people through the years. These stories I've related just happen to be mine. Here's one example to show I wasn't alone. A few years before I retired, I got a call from a colleague in another state.

She said, "I have a labor relations problem."

"What is it?" I asked.

"Well, I have an otherwise decent employee, Ms. Jones. Do you know her?"

"I don't think so, why?"

"She returned a government car full of grass clippings. I found out her husband used the car over the weekend to do a grass cutting job and he didn't clean the trunk after hauling the clippings away."

"Okay," I said.

"There's more. She also pawned the government laptop she'd taken home for the weekend. She told me she did this because her husband had gambling debts to pay. To cap it all off her defense for pawning the laptop was that she intended on redeeming it soon. Her proof that she would redeem it was that she had always done so in the past when she pawned the laptop and wasn't caught."

"So what is the problem?" I asked.

"Well, she is really nice and her husband is a creep. Should I protect her?"

I guess I am a meanie because I said, "Gloria, it is you or her. If you cover this up, you'll be the one in trouble."

Construction is Special

At EEOC we investigated construction unions and joint apprenticeship committees. They were tough nuts to crack because the best jobs were often reserved for the sons and nephews in the almost all-white union. Each local had a different dominant ethnic group. When I left EEOC, I didn't have any more construction union work. In 1993, though, the DOL decided to try again, but little had changed, and this department was still afraid to take on the issues of the construction unions.

We had one case in which the applicants were supposed to get five, ten, or fifteen points for re-applying for the second or third year in a row. They also got points for taking and passing algebra in high school. At this Joint Apprenticeship Committee we found that among the hundreds of applicants, the more a minority re-applied, the fewer points he received; however, the more times a white applicant applied, the more points he received. We found a situation in which a white applicant who had failed algebra twice received fifteen points while a minority applicant who had received an *A* in advanced algebra received no points at all. The facts were not in dispute, and no one could really tell us to back off; however, Washington just let the case lapse despite my being a pest about it.

*****

In the South, construction jobs are mostly non-union, and not surprisingly, minorities and women could get jobs. When they faced discrimination, it was usually a matter of inequality in pay. In the North, with better paying union jobs on the line, with the exception of laborers, minorities and women have historically had trouble getting into the jobs at all.

At an internal meeting once, I made a big mistake. I told the group that, apparently, crossing the Mason-Dixon Line northward made both minorities and women not as smart. Both groups were apparently smart enough to pass union admission tests in the South, but not in the North.

Later on, I explained the obvious joke, but this was during the "sensitive nineties" when nothing could be joked about; nor could the construction unions be forced into compliance.

Reports at DOL

The government work month is made up of 168 hours less time for sick leave, holidays, vacation, training, and any administrative time. Washington decided that cases were to average 80 hours each. Each person was to do two and a half cases per month (equaling 200 average hours) with no overtime.

The inference was that we were simple field people and apparently planning was out of our league. Yes, all we did was the analysis of employment and compensation systems. In our first six months under the new requirements of two and a half 80-hour cases per month, the most productive office (out of fifteen offices) reported completing one case per journeyman per month.

*****

Every month we had to send a narrative on the progress of cases to Washington. One of the four topics to be covered was *problems encountered*. However, the Regional Director instructed us that anyone who put any notations under *problems encountered* was a troublemaker and would be treated as disloyal to the program.

*****

On occasion, I had fun with the reports that had to be submitted. At DOL we had to send in a long quarterly report that covered many things the employees in the office did. One of the *things* was linkage agreements. Linkage agreements were never really defined. Moreover, I suspected that no one ever audited the number of linkage agreements we made. Our target number was expected to be at least five per quarter. When it came time to fill out the quarterly report, I always entered at least the target number, sometimes adding one or two more.

I attended a conference for admin affairs a couple years later. One speaker said, "The only one consistently hitting the linkage target is Duffy. Chuck, tell us how you do it."

I told them the truth. I told them I kept making up the numbers. Everyone laughed at my *joke*.

Eventually, linkage was defined and became auditable so I had to report the hard way—by actually checking to see how many we did.

There was also a useless narrative that went with the quarterly report. No District Director saw evidence that the narrative was ever read. For no good reason, I decided to turn the narrative into poetry. At least, that is the best spin I can put on what I did. Actually the *poetry* was made up of rhyming ditties that mocked and insulted some of our sillier rules. I continued this practice for several quarters.

One day, at another conference, I was seated next to the regional staffer who received and audited the quarterly reports. While the speaker droned on about some nonsense, the staffer, out of the blue, turned to me and from memory recited the first ten lines of my last narrative. Then he said, "If you keep this up and someone else reads those things, we're both screwed." Because of this and many other reasons besides, Don and I became good friends, and remain friends to this day. I think he liked watching me rave ineffectually at absurdity, and I love his understated sense of humor.

*****

I have always wondered why Sexual Harassment training is not called Anti-Sexual Harassment training. Be that as it may, we once had a Sexual Harassment training session that was interrupted by an awards luncheon a few blocks away that we walked to. Entertainment was provided including someone singing the song from the play *How to Succeed in Business Without Really Trying* in which the singer brags about hitting on all the secretaries all the time. I turned to Don and said, "And then back to Sexual Harassment training?"

Don looked at me and said, "If you don't behave, you'll have to wait in the car."

The Reagan Years

When the Reagan administration came in, its Labor Department appointees fought against awarding back-pay for group discrimination victims. Technically, back-pay couldn't be banned because it was a legally-required remedy, but it could be discouraged. First, we, as well as those in industry, were told how headquarters wouldn't enforce group back-pay cases. When that wasn't 100% successful because some companies kept agreeing to back-pay without the need for enforcement, we were told that the Agency Director needed to approve all agreements within forty-five days of receipt. If he/she failed to reject the agreement, it was approved. The message was this: Don't even bother sending back-pay cases forward for approval. Most, but not all, group back-pay cases went away.

Shortly after this, I managed to get a company to agree to back-pay without having to send the case for enforcement. I sent the case to Washington for the forty-five day review. Eighty or ninety days went by before I got a call from Washington. "The case is disapproved," they said.

"Too late. The company has already started payments. You are way past the forty-five days," I said.

That was the last group back-pay case I got through for several years.

The greatest Reagan era slap at the Civil Rights staff happened when he laid off or downgraded nearly half of us, nationwide. If the directions to cut back on enforcement were in any way subtle, the RIFS (Reductions in Force) were not. However, those of us not RIFed were paid every two weeks. Those who really lost out were the victims of discrimination whose discrimination, though found, was left un-remedied.

The worse case I ever experienced in which the victims were left un-remedied occurred in the early years of the Reagan administration. This happened in spite of the fact that it was one of the best cases a senior investigator (and also my office partner at DOD) at DOL put together. He both investigated and analyzed this case, which involved a savings and loan company. The two of us cut and pasted the report together. (In the days before word processors, we actually used scissors and tape to cut and paste the reports.) The write-up on this project was so long we actually crawled around on the floor putting it together. There were ten different groups of discrimination classes in this case. I have never heard of another case anywhere in which as many as ten classes were found. There was so much discrimination against so many people for so many reasons in so many ways that some individuals were in three or four classes.

It was common at this savings and loan for a minority woman to be underpaid for her position because of race, and then be refused a promotion because of gender, and then be further refused a transfer because of both race and sex.

We issued preliminary, and then formal findings, and then in due course were invited for negotiation to the offices of the law firm representing the savings and loan. Normally, we negotiated on our home turf, but this time we made an exception.

We walked into an opulent dark wood-paneled office with carpeting so plush I could have lost my shoes in it. The table was so thick it looked like one large tree had been used to manufacture it, and it was polished to a blinding glare. In walked the attorneys, each wearing a suit worth several thousands of dollars. We were greeted warmly, and the Cleveland sports teams and the weather were discussed. An ancient lady brought in a silver tea service and patterned china cups.

After enough pleasantries, their lead counsel said, "Would you like to discuss your case and where you want to go?"

I said, "No, we clearly laid out our findings in writing and this can be the meeting where we get your position." After a few more super polite "you go first" or "no, you", the lawyers agreed to talk.

The lawyer, pulled at the crease in his pants, crossed his legs, and rested his cup and saucer on his knee. He looked upward as if trying to think what to say. Finally, he sighed and said, "I guess if we had to state our position, it would be: Not one fucking dime."

"Well. That was very clear and concise," I said, "But are you aware that if you do not give us a heck of a lot more than a dime, we'll have to send the case for enforcement which will cost the S & L more in defense fees, PR, and interest? Then, you would still have to pay the back-pay."

"I know that's your position," he said, "But I and company defense lawyers everywhere have been assured by the Reagan Administration that Civil Rights cases are not going to be enforced. If the case isn't enforced, what incentive do we have to pay? We not only won't have to pay back-pay, but we'll have no defense costs and no press releases against us."

They were right. The case wasn't enforced. I don't remember if this case went into the great pile that awaited the Clinton years, but it didn't matter. By then, the S & L had gone under.

That case may have been my most humiliating defeat. However, I'm sure the many victims who went without remedy would have preferred bureaucratic defeat to what they got. What they got, instead, was a denial of a job or promotion, or even lower pay because of race or gender.

More DOL Cases

Normally, a case was investigated, sometimes by a team, the supervisor approved it, and findings were made and issued by the District Director. In a few cases, a long process of negotiation began. If settlement was close in the dollar amount agreement, the regional office or Headquarters was informed so that we'd know that the parameters were acceptable.

After the G.H.W. Bush years, I had several cases in which all the clearances were given and negotiations all but concluded when the Regional Director called and said he needed an increase in the dollar amount so he could achieve a particular figure of remedies for that quarter. This meant that I needed to return and get an increase in the settlement in spite of his prior approval, and in spite of my telling the company the case was ready, and sometimes in spite of the fact that there was no legal basis for the increase. If we failed to settle, often these cases wouldn't be enforced by SOL because of the lack of merit (SOL wanted slam-dunk cases) or because of the politics of the party in the White House. Once again, who cares about the victims?

Actually the victims were never the prime focus in any negotiation over back-pay and jobs. The main question being argued by both sides was whether or not there were victims at all.

*****

I had a case at DOL that was hung up at five hundred thousand dollars of back-pay. My instructions were to not settle for under five hundred thousand dollars ($500,000). A press release that says, "More than a half million dollars" sounds and spins better than any lower dollar amount. However, the company wouldn't budge.

Finally, my contact at the company in question said, "If you'll settle for $499,999, I'll throw in the extra dollar from my pocket, and you can do with it as you like."

That hooked me. We left the room; I took him aside, and asked him, "What's up?" I told him I assumed he feared a press release that said, "Over a half million dollars" as much as my bosses wanted it.

"No," he said. "You know the company is foreign owned. Any settlement at or above $500,000 needs approval overseas and U.S. management would rather fight for that one dollar in court than be embarrassed in front of the foreign management."

We settled for $499,999 on paper and put out an erroneous press release that we had settled for a half-million dollars.

*****

The sort of number manipulation mentioned above that we locals thought skillful was nothing compared to what Washington could do.

As the Reagan administration's policies took hold, we began, rightfully, taking heat from civil rights groups for falling back-pay awards. Conservative business groups praised us for the falling awards.

Nonetheless, it was decided to raise the claimed amounts of *dollar remedy* while also not disturbing industry by collecting more back-pay. But how to do this? The solution was simple. *Dollar remedy* and back-pay had always been synonymous. Henceforth, we were instructed that we must count back-pay, the first year projected earnings of any victims scheduled to be hired, and the administrative and training costs *estimated by the company* as likely to be incurred carrying out the remedy agreement to be the *dollar remedy*. Dollar remedy went up; back-pay stayed the same or even decreased, and the problem was solved. One Regional Director forever after always called the dollar remedy that was not back-pay *funny money*.

When the Clinton administration came in, they found many years-old enforcement cases backed up. Our lawyers had had no grounds to drop them, but no approval to process them, either.

Is it 75 Cents or 95 Cents on the Dollar?

In my opinion the liberals and the conservatives both have it wrong when it comes to many EEO issues. The left claims that women only make seventy-five cents on the dollar compared to men, and this needs to be remedied. The figure of seventy-five cents may be true, but it totally ignores education, job title, and experience. If, perhaps, the point is that women *should* be represented in each job men hold, in roughly the same numbers and experience, that would be correct. But they aren't, and some of this is free will, not discrimination. There could be a disagreement with societal choices made by large groups of people, but there can't be an accusation against an individual employer of discrimination because of the lower pay structure for admin assistants compared to engineers.

Conservatives point out that when comparing women to men of the same experience, education, and tenure, women make ninety-five percent as much. This gap of five percent is trivial, they claim.

Earlier, I mentioned that by the time I retired most HR/EEO personnel were either young, a minority, a woman, or a combination of any of these three groups. I gave a talk on *"What's new"* to such a group just before I left the government. Coincidentally, I had been diagnosed with Bell's palsy the day before the scheduled speech. I started with the bit, "I'm from the government and here to help you" and followed up by telling them that I had Bell's palsy which froze half of my face so that they'd get the treat of hearing from a government employee who was physically incapable of talking out of both sides of his mouth. This group loved anything that was a government put-down.

One other day, I spoke again to another similar group of HR-types. This time my speech happened to follow a speech by someone who reported that women **really** made ninety-five percent as much as men. During my speech (*What's New*), I told the group about an hourly race case in which the minorities were paid nineteen dollars an hour compared to the whites, who were paid twenty dollars an hour for the same job. "So," I said, "We dropped the case because the difference was so little."

Hands went up. "That's two thousand dollars a year," these touchy souls cried. "That's discrimination!"

"Well," I said, "The minorities make ninety-five percent as much as the whites. How is that different from the 'no problem' when the situation affects women?" Then I confessed. There never was such a minority case. However, I think I'd made my point.

Traveling some more

For my job, I not only flew on the little Brower Airways, but I flew all over the United States. My biggest regret is that I wasn't supposed to keep frequent flier miles. While federal employees can now keep frequent flier miles, and even back then some did, it wasn't allowed.

Allegedly the lack of frequent flier miles helped the government get a great corporate rate on tickets. This great rate, however, resulted in the worst seats. I often sat in the last row, middle seat in which the seat only reclines into the rear restroom wall.

Leaving O'Hare to come home one Friday night, a co-worker and I waited to board a sixty-passenger plane. The gate agent walked to the microphone next to the door at the jet-way. Per usual, we heard: "We will board by row from the rear forward." First, she said, "First class can now board." Then she followed with, "Persons traveling with small children can board." She added, "Those in wheelchairs or needing assistance can board." She said, "Those in the mileage club with gold, silver, bronze, and of course, with platinum elite status, can board at any time."

Finally, "Now we are ready for general boarding."

Ron and I looked around the waiting area and at each other, and then laughed. We were the only passengers on a full plane who weren't special. We were the general boarders.

*****

On another Friday night, we (passengers) sat on a plane at LaGuardia waiting in a long line for takeoff. All westbound traffic was held up because of storms coming in, but eastbound traffic could go. This meant that there had to a break in the line to let the eastbound traffic through to the runway. Sitting on the terminal side of the plane, I was in the last plane before the break. I watched a small plane taxi through. Then a medium-sized plane came through, and I noted how its wings filled the gap between my plane and the one behind us more so than the previous, smaller plane. Finally, a large plane approached. I thought it was surely an optical illusion because this plane didn't look like it would fit through. Just as the thought formed itself--WHAM! We were hit so hard our tail was off the waiting runway, and our tail rudder crumpled.

The offending plane had its wing ripped, and since this is where fuel is stored, aviation fuel spilled all over. We were told that we needed to stay on the plane *for your safety.*

Fumes from the fuel filled the plane, but nothing ignited. We sat on the tarmac for forty-five minutes or so while lights were set up and pictures taken. Then, apparently for our safety, a metal stairway was rolled out over the fuel mixed with water, and we disembarked into the rain as the front came in. Lightning hit at the other end of the runway, but was headed our way.

We all made it to the terminal unscathed, but cranky. Because it was so late, the airline only had one representative. She told us that the airline didn't intend to call in relief just to get us out that night. The angry passengers, now a mob, surged toward the airline representative, who called over a local cop. When the officer heard the story, he sided with the mob.

At about this time, I and about other ten passengers noticed a flight for Cleveland that was delayed, and had not yet taken off. I made it on the run, and don't know what happened to the rest of the passengers.

The following morning I looked in the *Plain Dealer* but never saw any coverage about the incident.

Starting Glass Ceilings and Returning to Back-Pay

In the last couple years of working for the government, I was able to be assigned to both national and regional training, teaching, and team-leading assignments on cases of Glass Ceiling and Compensation analyses. This meant that we'd either do the training or the reviews throughout the country if it involved a large corporation's practices. The practices we would focus on included the whole professional and managerial staff's compensation, promotion, recruitment, and hiring to see if there were any formal or informal barriers to advancement of women and/or minorities.

I love training, and I love the focus on whole systems; I also like the big, systemic look. Unlike EEOC, which is the place for those cases covering situations like "my foreman is nasty to me because I am _____" (a woman, a minority, over forty, of this religious persuasion, of this national origin, disabled, or a veteran), OFCCP (Department of Labor) mostly looks at groups and systems. Also, this was the only time that I remember that we were allowed to do other than the lowest common denominator training, which is related to the reverse incentive systems mentioned later in Part II. Lowest common denominator training is basically training that has to allow for the least capable employee at every level being able to understand the training. For once, this was not the case.

Although Glass Ceilings reviews started during the (first) President Bush's administration, it took until the middle of the Clinton era before we were able to go into a new area like professional and managerial compensation with a broad focus and new approach. Before that, it was the late seventies since we had seen progressive changes. To me, the new approach was extra legal, that is, meaning that it wasn't illegal, but it also wasn't proven in court. We got very rough indicators of salary problems and maybe added one level of failed rebuttal, and then we went to the company and said, "Why not save yourself the hassle and settle now?"

The company could fight, and maybe win, but they often knew they looked bad. If they spent a lot of money on a defense, they could still lose in court. They could also lose in the court of public opinion, or even because private group litigants could enter the picture.

On a practical level, it usually worked like this: we'd begin a Corporate Management Review, which was known as a Glass Ceiling review. We'd get compensation data on thousands of professional and managerial employees. Investigators would ask: "What is the main way you divide salaries?"

Company officials would usually say: "By pay grade or by title."

We'd organize the workforce by pay grade (or title) and also by gender and race. In some cases, we would say: "The women make less at each grade (and by a statistically significant amount due to the large numbers involved). What is the main cause of differing pay with grade?"

The company representatives would often answer: "Evaluations." After all, they believed that they were a merit-based pay company. Often, they made the assumption that they were a merit-based pay company and never even checked to see if it was true before sending the data in.

This excuse ("we are a merit pay company") put a company under instant scrutiny because the first rule investigators were taught is: You are investigating relative practice, not policy. In the early days of EEOC, this wasn't true. Many of the policies, at that time, were illegal. Later on, however, woe to the company who had fair policies, but never checked to see if the policies translated to the practice. It was so common for companies to not follow their own policies that we were not shocked when we saw that they had ignored them. We just checked to see if by not following the policy, the company had caused relative harm in practice to the aggrieved party (typically women or minorities). If not, we ignored the company's failure to follow its own policy. It wasn't a matter of feeling bad for the company. We knew that if we found against the company simply for not following its own policy, when the company lawyers got involved, they'd invoke the legal equivalent of basketball's "no harm, no foul" rule.

Notwithstanding the policy/practice issue, for the first time in twenty years, we had the "shooting fish in a barrel" situation we had experienced in simpler times when some companies claimed that because women aren't the main breadwinners, we don't pay them the same as men. This time we were able to crack the pay systems at the mid- and upper white-collar levels. Previously, it had been impossible because there were so few women and minorities in these jobs, and one-on-one comparisons had to be made. In the nineties, however, we finally had a critical mass of women and minorities in professional and managerial jobs, other than just what was seen at universities.

I know I was more into this than most people. We also had a green light from Washington. Joe Dubray, the Regional Director from Philadelphia, spearheaded the effort. I had a merry band of co-conspirators on my teams. There was no shortage of large companies from which to choose.

The reason I know I was maybe too far into these cases was because no one else, even on my true believers' team, seemed as excited as I when I got a case that allowed me to develop what I called "dream graphs." From my earliest days at EEOC, I had wished for the perfect class case. A perfect case would show with one or two graphs (dream graphs) a major case by simplifying it down to the level of those early we-don't-hire-women cases.

The case occurred at a Fortune 100 company headquartered in New York City. The person to whom I was making the case was normally called an EVP of Human Resources, but had what I thought was the humorous title of President, People Division, but I digress. With lawyers and experts all around, there is about a ten-minute timeframe to present the case before everyone jumps in with, "Oh yeah, what about this?"

My fantasy-turned-reality graphs had pink and blue lines representing women and men respectively and they showed a great case. We had asked the company: "How do you first divide pay?"

Their answer: "By grade."

We followed with: "What is the biggest determinant of pay in grade?"

Their answer: "Evaluations."

I was able to produce one graph that showed average pay by grade and gender. As the grades went up, so did the average male and female pay. The problem for the company was that the blue line, which represented the male pay, continued to be five to fifteen thousand dollars higher than the pink line, representing female pay, from the lowest grade to the highest grade. Then we produced the evaluations graph, which we overlaid on the salary graph. The pink line for evaluations was about a half point higher than the blue line at each grade. Busted! Presentation over.

The President of the People Division and I just stared at each other while the arguing began and then continued for another hour. I heard how we wouldn't win; how we'd be beat in court; how outside counsel knew the Secretary of Labor; how the data was wrong; how the presentation was too simplistic. There were several more meetings, and a large settlement was worked out.

Of course, after the George W. Bush regime took hold, such cases went the way of the back-pay cases of the Reagan years. While the old DuBray method of compensation analysis did not come back into usage in the Obama administration, another system did. This system, which is both simpler and complex at the same time, is as follows:

Roughly, if women or minorities in a pay group average either 2% or $2000 a year less than men, the case is investigated in great depth at a significant cost to the company

*****

Some of the Glass Ceiling cases had amusing elements. No wild behavior, just amusing moments.

We had a National Office representative come out to close one of the first Glass Ceiling cases. Her name was Jude. At one point in the review, with just our team present, she was complaining. With silent apologies to the Beatles, I said, "Hey Jude. Don't be afraid. Take that sad song and make it better. Uh huh." She didn't get it, but everyone else and I rolled our eyes, and felt so old.

One of the things we wanted to accomplish in those early reviews was the training of the local senior people who had never done a Glass Ceiling review. A key nontechnical aspect of the training was sensitizing our staff to the delicate proper approaches to senior corporate officials. This didn't always work out.

While I didn't attend this review at a Catholic institution of higher learning, I relate this story here. It was a pre-award contract review, and to the team leader's horror, a team member asked what the award was for. The Brother who was President of the institution spoke some jargon about airborne laser technology and air-to-ground application. The team member paused, and then said, "Hmmm." Then he exclaimed, "Oh my God. You are developing a death ray. A Catholic school developing a death ray!" The team leader apologized and agreed that they were there only to check EEO in personnel actions, not pass moral judgments. Nonetheless, I heard from the local congressman.

*****

One Glass Ceiling review I led was at a cookie company. They left their brand as snacks in all meeting rooms. Joining us at one meeting was an attorney brought in by the company and known to be a barracuda by the local staff. She was always ready to exploit any weakness and start a fight, I was told.

Several of the people had stuffed their mouths when one of the DOL staff members picked that time to pipe up, "I'm a diabetic and you put sugars on your cookie labels, but not carbs. That's misleading and wrong. You should re-label everything." (In such a situation, the last thing needed was a fight over something irrelevant to the job at hand. The job, by the way, was ensuring equal employment, not food labeling.) With that, the barracuda was off to the races (to mix metaphors) with this issue. It took a day to get the focus back on EEO.

*****

Other than the big money cases, my favorite Glass Ceiling story concerns the Japanese-owned steel company that we reviewed in Medinio, Indiana. As we piled into two cars to drive from the local office to the company, the local Director turned to his Deputy and told her to stay on his tail so she wouldn't get lost. The Deputy said, "Don't worry, Phil. I'll stick to you like a dirty shirt."

When we arrived, the president of the company introduced himself as Yirio Tinirio. Through the translator, I asked him where he was from, and found out that he was from Tokyo. Perhaps it isn't funny in a cross cultural way, but I had trouble keeping a straight face at this meeting in Medinio with the rhyming Yirio Tinirio from Tokyo.

After the typical greetings, our representative gave the standard Secretary of Labor speech about glass ceilings. Throughout it all, the translator translated his speech into Japanese. Our representative then gave a booklet on breaking the glass ceiling to the president, who looked at the earnest translator. The president had a puzzled look on his face so the translator, still translating the speaker's words, also with his hands made the universal hourglass figure that symbolizes women. Then, with his right arm level, he made a ceiling, and with his left arm, he punched at and then through it. The president smiled, and let out a large, "Aha!" Without pause, our speaker continued.

After these opening ceremonies, the theatre of the absurd continued. Typically, the president left, and the EVP of HR came on to deal with specifics. As is often usual in steel plants, the EVP was a large, beefy man. The main point he wanted to make was that he had played tackle for the world famous football factory down the road from the company. Then he left after turning us over to the tiny, young, short-haired woman, who actually ran the plant. We didn't realize this at first. Despite her diminutiveness, Bunny had a deep voice and seemed no-nonsense in her manner, but all in all, she was actually quite agreeable.

During the review, I was invited back to her office for some discussion, and while there, saw a plastic cafeteria serving tray mounted on her wall. It was an award to Bunny "Boom Boom" Bitcowski for being number one Slammer. When asked, she explained that at her college in northern

Michigan there was a winter sled run in which everyone took cafeteria trays and raced in the snow. I always liked she had that award displayed. It, as well as pictures of her kids, dominated the room. Most other HR types, if they have any other ego wall decorations, have industry awards.

*****

Sometimes company representatives would be the ones to blurt out irrelevancies that got everyone off point. The companies had no real reason to sensitize their people to us other than to impress us with their commitment to diversity at the upper levels. Nonetheless, they were almost always naturally smooth. Perhaps they told their people to act this way. The one exception to this, at least the one that stands out in my mind, was a presentation made by several division presidents at a company that made pharmaceutical drugs and medical devices. The topic of the presentation was the business forecast as it related to future staffing. Since future staffing is an employment-related topic, we were still on topic.

One division president began his presentation to his CEO and EVP of Human Resources and us. After a minute or two, he became very animated and enthusiastic as he turned to the subject of overseas demand. "Trend analysis confirms that Japanese hypertension will continue to rise for the next several years, and we will be able increase sales of our product by forty-five percent as the Japanese blood pressure problems continue," he said. As I ponder this, I realize it wasn't so much what he said as the fact he was wringing his hands, running in place with glee, and beaming maniacally. I think he expected everyone present to stand and cheer. All of us, government and industry types, sat mute and as devoid of expression as within our individual control. He seemed to be the only one in the room who did not understand his joy at making a profit on the projected misery of others.

After he left the room, the VP of Public Affairs tried to assured us that the Division President's callous presentation of the facts was strictly a coping mechanism for a sensitive soul whose job, day after day, was to try to provide treatment for those who suffer.

CONSULTING

After I retired, I became a part-time consultant. This is known by some government types as *going to the dark side*. I didn't market myself because I didn't feel like working full-time. I also didn't write Affirmative Action Plans. I could have and I have, but I think companies should update their own AAPs.

According to my son-in-law, the lack of marketing and AAP writing weren't the only things that limited my consulting. He told me that I had to talk slowly if I intended to bill by the hour. While I am neither from New York nor New Jersey, apparently I still talk too fast (since he is from Oklahoma).

When he gave me the good advice about talking slowly (and yes, he was smiling), I was reminded of the old Bob and Ray comedy routine in which Ray is frustrated with Bob who is playing... Harlow... P... Whitcomb, ... the... President.... of.... the... slow... talkers... of... America.

*****

Usually I am hired by counsel or HR when there is either a problem with the government or there is an anticipated problem. If I am called in early enough, I can usually prevent problems. If, however, I'm called in late, I'm doing damage control. Only one company has wanted to hire me to help them avoid compliance with the law. On that occasion, we quickly fired each other. Everyone else that I have worked for just wanted to know how, on a practical basis, to comply with the law.

One company hired me by mistake, much to their good fortune. Since they were the smallest company I had worked with, I asked them how they found out I was consulting and why they hired me. "Because you are the only sensible government person we have dealt with," they said. Like the entertainer milking the applause, I asked the President and VP of Human Resources what made them think I was so sensible.

The VP said, "Because you signed off on closing out our last review." The only institutional memory they had of that review was the closeout letter.

When I researched the last review, I found that I had signed a finding against them for discriminating against women; had negotiated a settlement with jobs and over $100,000 in back-pay; and had demanded four semi-annual reports showing they were being compliant (good). Yes, when all that was done, I had signed a *sensible* letter closing the case.

The current case was a minority hiring case. The first thing the President wanted me to do was confirm how unreasonable the investigator had been. After looking at the case file, I told the President that the investigator had done a good job and had drawn the only possible conclusions based on the data the company had given him. The HR VP asked me how the conclusion could be right when they were based on company data which was partially wrong. Risking future billable hours, I asked if the company's defense was going to be, essentially, "You are stupid for having believed us." To the company's credit, they saw my point, and we went to work.

Recalling the earlier story regarding the French boss whose team was delighted because I told him no, I had one consulting case that was a similar situation. In fact, the case lasted two hours. My sole job was to give my opinion as to whether something was legal, to which I said, "No." I was then asked by the outside counsel to get on a conference call with the inside counsel, HR, VP, Divisional President (all of these were in the U.S.), and the CEO, who was not based in the U.S. because the company was foreign-owned. It was clear that I was to be used just this once to give my opinion to the CEO because no one else who worked for him dared. I obliged. The CEO fumed, but the U.S. division was able to stay out of trouble with the government.

*****

Just as advice by investigators can be boiled down, most consultants' advice in the EEO field can be simplified. Most companies will say that they just want to know the rules. However, simple advice is usually more helpful than the explanation of some small rule. Sure, advice can be oversimplified until it is then no longer useful: Do good; avoid evil. The most useful advice I have is simply this: Do your internal audit before you get a notice of review or complaint. Yes, there are others things to say that should be obvious that go with that sentence. Fortunately from the standpoint of a consultant, if they were that obvious, there would be little need for consultants at all.

So here goes the simple advice. When you do an internal audit (that is, a statistical look at success in applications, hiring, promotion, compensation, and terminations by race and gender), do not forget to react when the audit shows something is a little off. If you are hiring minority clericals way under their application rate, don't say it is probably an anomaly. Check the prior year or two. If women in marketing are paid less or promoted less rapidly than men, don't guess that they perform less well or have less experience or education. Instead, check. And then check to see that the quality women lack is possessed by the men. And then further check that the job requirement that the women lack but men have is valid or, put another way, a skill, knowledge, or ability needed to do the job is actually there.

That's it. Do internal audits and you'll have fewer complaints from EEOC or the state agencies. You'll be better able to answer the ones you get. Eventually, you may have fewer reviews. This is because the DOL has, for the last few years, scheduled reviews based on your relative employment profile compared to other like companies. If you have had good internal audits, your profile may be better and thus less likely to cause an audit. Certainly, if you are audited, the review will go better and faster if you have done internal audits.

Part II

Statistics

Context

It is now hard to imagine, but forty years ago equal employment and equal educational opportunity were controversial and hotly debated social topics. While the analogy might not be perfect, a modern parallel might be global warming and energy issues. Like global warming, lack of equal employment was thought by many not to be a problem that existed. Progress towards any issue can be stalled completely if there is room to deny that the problem exists. Continuing with the analogy of global warming and energy issues, some of the roadblocks on the climate change issue are questions such as the following:

Is global warming real?

Is it caused by man?

If it is real, do we care who caused it except to the extent that it might inform us as to how to deal with it?

To the extent that oil is expensive, running out, and frequently comes from unstable or unfriendly overseas suppliers, does global warming have to exist before we need to do something about the oil issue?

Or, do we need to drill, baby, drill?

Even after BP and the Gulf of Mexico fiasco?

Is Green technology something we need to do to save ourselves, or is it something we need to do to save money, or is it something to just ignore?

Can coal be made more non-polluting in a cost-effective way?

Is nuclear energy the way to go?

Is it safe enough to operate and dispose of?

We had the same sort of arguments over EEO forty years ago.

Polls

Obviously polls regarding attitudes on gender and race in employment and higher education done from the late 1960s were not conducted to be reviewed later for this book. Nonetheless, I include a sampling of several that illustrate my present purpose. (All polls cited here were obtained from searches of the *I*poll database provided by the Roper Center for Public Opinion Research at the University of Connecticut.)

First, I'll highlight some polls on race issues.

In March 1970, sixteen years after the *Brown versus The Board of Education* decision desegregated schools with "all deliberate speed", the Harris Poll asked 1600 white adults: "As you know, the U.S. Supreme Court has ruled that public schools which are segregated must become integrated now without further delay. In general, do you tend to approve or disapprove of the ruling for integration now by the Supreme Court?"

> The results:
> 48% approved
> 38% disapproved
> 14% were not sure

By 1978 things had changed. When the Harris Poll for the National Conference of Christians and Jews asked 1673 white adults: "Would you like to see the children in your family go to school with black children or not?"

The results:
32% said yes
20% volunteered that they "already do"
30% said it makes no difference
14% said no
4% were not sure

In July 1971, seven years after the Civil Rights Act of 1964 banned job discrimination, the Harris Poll asked 1600 adults of all races: "Are Blacks discriminated against in getting white-collar jobs?"

The results:
18% said a great deal
27% said somewhat
18% said only a little
31% said not at all
6% were not sure

To me, being discriminated against "only a little" is like being only a little pregnant. I read the 1971 poll as saying sixty-three percent of adults of all races feel blacks are being discriminated against from a lot to a little. Worse, since six percent of the respondents weren't sure whether or not blacks were being discriminated against, the sixty-three percent is actually sixty-seven percent of those with an opinion.

Fast forward to 2010. Nineteen percent of African Americans aged 25 to 29 had a minimum of a four-year college degree. This was great progress, but remember this number in two contexts. First, in 2010 thirty-nine percent of whites aged 25 to 29 had four-year college degrees. Second, and as a segue to gender, of 25 to 29 year-old African Americans with at least a four-year degree sixty-three percent are women and thirty-seven percent are men.

Now, look at a poll result on gender issues.

For the Virginia Slims American Women's Poll in August 1970, the Harris Poll asked 1012 *men*: "Do women stand an equal chance with the men they work with in becoming executives or not?" Notice that the question begins with "Do" and not "Should". The men responded:

32% women had an equal chance
59% women had less than an equal chance
9% were not sure

Again, fast forward to 2010. Thirty-six percent of women aged 25 to 29 have a minimum of a four-year degree compared to twenty-eight percent of men in that age group. The Pew Research Center, in a poll released August 17th 2011 and conducted from March 15th to the 29th, 2011 found the following: Seventy-seven percent of Americans say college is necessary for women while only sixty-eight percent say it is necessary for men.

The Many Issues Raised

Gender

At the time of the 1970 poll, debate raged over whether women should be allowed in jobs where they lifted weight; over whether the federal government could overrule state law on weight-lifting; over whether pregnancy discrimination should be its own category, and different from gender discrimination. It was at least another decade before sexual harassment was considered. Did it cover harassment by both genders? Against either gender? If we have to let *girls* into college, do we have to let them into programs in which there historically haven't been that many women? Must we pay women the same as men in the same job? Even if the woman isn't the "breadwinner"?

Race

On race issues, the need for and the legitimacy of Affirmative Action was debated and still is. Was it needed at all? Are goals, quotas? If it is needed, could it be required without a finding of discrimination? Could the government tell a private employer what to do? What of customer preference? How could a black man possibly sell cars to a white customer base? Wouldn't requiring that cause the compliant auto dealer to go out of business? Does seniority in union contracts trump the effect of last-in, first-out when minorities are always last in? Assuming country clubs are private associations and exempt from laws requiring equal admission rules, does this impact companies that pay country club dues?

Disability

The dynamics of race and gender issues were soon seen as parallel to disability issues and handicap rules. For more than ten years before the Americans with Disabilities Acts was signed, the government was enforcing something called Sections 503 and 504 of the Vocational Rehabilitation Act. It covered all federal contractors and grantees. We needed to know: What is a handicap? Which handicapped people are covered for what jobs? What is reasonable accommodation? If a handicapped person had to be able to perform major elements of the job in question, what are the major elements of a job?

Overall

Some of these issues are issues today, but I would guess the answers we worked out as a society are taken for granted by today's college senior. Without taking sides on the global warming issues, like EEO issues, I can imagine that in fifteen years or so my granddaughters will laugh at the idea that a popular attitude in the early twenty-first century was the following: "If I want to pay for the gas for my SUV that gets twelve miles to the gallon, that's my right."

Now, as we've evolved more, although of limited impact as of yet in federal law, how do we treat issues of homosexuality in the workplace (anti-gay discrimination)? Is marriage a civil right? Is marriage primarily a religious issue into which secular society should not intervene? If gays can marry, why not allow brother-to-brother or sister-to- sister marriage?

"Just Ban Discrimination and Everything will be Fine"

I receive many "oldies" e-mails with video or slide shows. Wasn't it great back then? Sure, these are mostly about prices or music, but when they stray into social areas, they display nostalgia for a time that never was. This blind eye is not turned on purpose. Rather, my friends in middle class, white America remember the old days the way these e-mails portray it. I'm fairly sure minorities do not remember it that way.

Yet this group false memory syndrome isn't just the musings of middle class whites. To them, it *was* the good old days.

However, many other subtexts were at play. I'm not sure that I can weave them all together and make one point. While one shouldn't pretend that we didn't have any problems before the civil rights laws were passed, one should also not pretend that the civil rights laws were clear and made it all better.

For example, the income tax laws, as well as an amendment allowing an income tax, have been on the books for almost one hundred years. Then, a bit later, a graduated income tax was legislated. If that should have made taxes clear, why are taxes still so confusing and changeable? Civil rights law is similarly confusing and contradictory.

Civil Rights Contradictions and Confusions

African Americans

Historic discrimination in the African American community exists based on skin shade.

Who is black is itself a crazy question. Most *blacks* in the U.S. are not black in skin color. Scientists can not find race at the DNA level, yet we obsess over the issue.

We understand the phrase *passing as white,* but it makes no more literal sense than having one drop of African American heritage and being considered black as in the old South.

If one is black, but not born in the U.S., then one has no U.S. slave ancestors. Does that make a difference? If so, what?

Even today we've heard of people being arrested for *DWBs* (driving while black), a take-off on DWI. Certainly no one should be pulled over just because of their skin color, but just as certainly, no one should assume that just because they are black and pulled over, it was because they are black.

As an idea, reparation for slavery is considered dead, I think, but when it was alive, we had lots of issues. Did the Civil War dead pay the reparations with their lives? Does welfare, going disproportionately, to African Americans count? If it counts as reparations, why does it exist for those people who are not descendents of slaves? Would descendents of non-African American post-Civil War immigrants have to pay? Would Barack Obama and Colin Powell be left out because neither had a U.S. slave ancestor? Was Affirmative Action the reparation?

Most of us have heard of illegal, under the Fair Housing Law, but widely accepted methods employed to stop *blockbusting*. Blockbusting is the practice in which one block at a time becomes occupied by blacks or other minorities—usually first as renters—converting all white segregation into all black segregation. In the medium and long term, this benefits no one as landlords' profits shrink, homes are sold, and housing values also drop. Shaker Heights, Ohio and Oak Park, Illinois have tried various methods to let integration happen without re-segregation occurring. Yet to accomplish this, realtors, city, state, and federal officials have had to ignore several well-meaning laws.

Hispanics and Native Americans

Hispanics and African Americans compete for the "top" minority group. This affects money to community programs, and census issues. It led to redefining self-identification at the Census Bureau and on EEO forms. Some Spanish-speaking Caribbean islands and South American countries have a large population whose ancestors were African slaves. Are these people Hispanic?

There are various sub-categories of Hispanics. Puerto Ricans are citizens automatically. They cluster in different parts of the country and have a slightly different culture from Mexican Americans, some of whom are illegal immigrants. Cubans are in another category, and are categorized under the "wet foot, dry foot" policy. Those who manage to seek asylum in the United States and actually set foot on land are not returned to Cuba. If they are intercepted at sea, they are returned to their native land of Cuba. On the other hand, Haitians are not afforded this policy, and as such, are deported regardless of whether found on land or at sea. Central and South Americans are a different issue as is the differing social classes within any of these groups.

In the southwest United States, an Apache living just north of the Rio Grande is a Native American. His cousin, who comes here to work, living just south of the Rio Grande is classified as a Hispanic.

Portuguese are not considered Hispanic. Yet they share the Iberian Peninsula with Spain, have a similar language to Spanish, and the people of the largest country in South America, Brazil, speak Portuguese.

Asians

Even in the mostly successful Asian community, there are subcategories and subcategories of subcategories. Many Japanese Americans in the continental U.S. were interned during World War II (compared with relatively few German or Italian Americans). Not all, however, were so treated. In spite of their numbers and geographic closeness to the war zone, those who lived in Hawaii were not interned (further proof to me of the insanity of the internments that occurred on the mainland). When reparations were discussed, Japanese Americans, who lived in Hawaii, and their children, got less involved than those who lived on the mainland.

I have been told by a participant's father that in the San Francisco-Oakland area that there are public "Asian Leagues" for basketball. Public support is illegal, but condoned by all. Further, it is understood that the leagues are supposed to be for Japanese Americans only because of their average height.

Gender and Race

Some felt that the gender discrimination law was just meant to weaken race discrimination enforcement.

Rampant sexism exists among some African American males. "Machismo" certainly isn't the Spanish word for gender equality.

We demand nondiscrimination by law but champion "diversity" as a good idea. However, when studies are done, and Glass Ceiling reviews are done we find "diversity" ends somewhere below the VP level. What makes women or minorities successful near the top is blending in, that is, acting, dressing, speaking, and educating themselves, just like those already at the top of the corporate culture. What is more, that culture is not a monolith, but, rather, slightly different at each large institution. Also, as the person approaches the top of any one large company, the culture, or what is called "fit", in high level jobs changes. The "diversity" we seek at the top may be gender or race related, but there is much more to "fit" than race or gender.

Here is one equal employment related example. It is much more common in sales, marketing, or advertising to meet a woman in an upper level position dressed in a short red skirt and wearing long earrings than it is in the fields of engineering or accounting. An equally qualified woman in a short red skirt and large earrings might not be able to rise to the top jobs in accounting or engineering at the same company, but gender, per se, would not necessarily be the reason. Of course, this same comparison can often be said of males in these respective fields.

Affirmative Action versus Quotas and *Fair versus Equal*

A fact not widely known outside those directly involved at DOD, HEW, and later, DOL, was that we regulated business mostly under executive orders, not laws. That is, Title VII of the Civil Rights Act of 1964 forbade discrimination by law. Federal courts would backup that law, but executive orders aren't *law*. Instead, they were government contract regulations. If a business wanted a federal contract or subcontract, when the contract was signed, the contract that was signed indicated that there was not to be any discrimination against women and minorities. If there was discrimination, then the penalty was corporate-wide loss of federal contracts, but not federal court orders.

The corporate-wide loss of contracts was our only penalty for refusal to change ways if we went to hearing and won. This led to the charge that we were using an atomic bomb when a fly swatter would do. It was true that if a company had a no minority hiring policy across all divisions, we would debar them from future contracts and take away the current ones. It is also true that if one foreman in one plant refused one woman overtime for reasons of gender, the ultimate penalty was still loss of all corporate-wide contracts, presently and in the future. In practice this meant that we almost never took individual cases to trial, and that companies settled before trial if they thought they would lose.

My two years at EEOC focused solely on equal employment opportunity cases; otherwise, all the other civil rights cases I worked on were both Affirmative Action and equal employment cases. That is, we did a general review of the treatment of employees (and students at HEW) and also checked affirmative action efforts. Affirmative Action has been like a hot iron to the rear of conservatives who call affirmative action "quota hiring." Why then (in Part I) don't I dwell on Affirmative Action?

There are two reasons. First, inside the field, I have held a heretical position for twenty-five years. *Bigot* or *racist* were the terms used in the civil rights community for people who did not have a blind allegiance to the idea that Affirmative Action was always good. Even President Clinton's "Mend it, don't end it," was widely seen (correctly, I believe) as a tactical position meant to diffuse criticism and allow some Affirmative Action to continue. In the past few years, however, moderate voices have been saying what I have thought for a quarter century.

That is, the sons and daughters of the upper middle class should not be getting special treatment regardless of race or gender. In college admissions the selective private colleges have always effectively given special treatment to the children of physicians, lawyers, bankers, and other well-to-do people. That isn't part of this debate. However, affirmative action in college admissions means selective schools also now give additional special treatment to the children of well-to-do minorities--those who do not even need it. Furthermore, this means that selective schools have nearly frozen out lower middle class whites.

In higher education, certain admission percentages were to be met regardless of test scores. This was soon banned, and the courts moved to allowing race as a *plus* factor in admissions. Even race as a plus factor has been modified over the years. The trouble is *race* is meaningless without *class*. How well off the student's family is and how good the high school from which the applicant comes predicts more than race when it comes to college suitability.

In private employment *affirmative action* is not the term that should be used for remedying discrimination. If an employer has discriminated, change the systemic problems, and find the victims to give them remedy. We should vigorously pursue discrimination to end it; however, we should not call the remedy *affirmative action.*

Second, those outside the field do not understand that affirmative action means different things depending on whether the discussion is public or private contracts, public or private employment, provision of services, admission to college, or construction or non-construction employment. It even means different things depending on which decade is being discussed. The rules and guidance from the Supreme Court are very different in 2010 than they were in 1970s or 1980s.

Occasionally I get asked by friends: "Do you favor Affirmative Action?"

If I answer, "It depends," and then launch into a long discussion of variables, eyes glaze over. Here is a mini-eyes-glazed-over discussion of affirmative action problems in construction and in college admission.

Pre-1975 construction companies often were given "make up goals" on top of normal goals when they inevitably failed to meet either their female 6.9% or local labor market minority percentage goal. It is hard to argue that these were not quotas except that failing to meet these quotas per se didn't cause the company to be in any trouble. Minority and female-owned companies often have a certain percentage of a public contract set aside for them. Everyone knows of the rampant abuse that has occurred here. Phony companies or companies that only enrich one or two persons have been the norm.

Conversely, the Affirmative Action I not only worked with, but also still agree with, required an employer compare his or her workforce percentages of women and minorities in similar occupational groupings to the percentages of qualified women and minorities available to do that work in the company's normal recruiting area. For example, if a company is hiring chemists, it needs to see whether the current percentage of female chemists is more, less, or the same as the percentage available in the recruiting area. If the employed percentage is significantly lower than those available, then there needs to be a pledge to hire women in at least the percentage of those available until what is called full utilization is reached. Companies never tired of pointing out that under utilization or full utilization, but not overutilization, was possible.

Quota hiring is actually expressly forbidden in the affirmative action regulations. This doesn't mean that a lazy personnel manager hasn't ever gone out and hired unqualified minorities and women to meet a goal. It does mean that this is a stupid, unlawful thing to do. It is stupid because once unqualified persons are hired as if they were qualified, then they must be paid, promoted, and disciplined like everyone else. Hiring the unqualified is always trouble in the long run.

It has always been unnecessary in the short run, too. I am only talking about non-construction employment here, but I never heard of any company anywhere in the U.S. ever found guilty of violating the affirmative action regulations for simple failure to reach a goal.

Since President Clinton's "Mend it. Don't end it." Policy started around 1993, all that ever happens, if a company hasn't set needed goals, is that it is asked to from now on. As long as the company agrees to set a goal, the government goes away happy. Any good faith answer, such as the ultimate "we weren't hiring," given two to five years later when the government follows up, will suffice.

This is not to minimize the positive effect of having companies focus on both recruiting from nontraditional sources and validating job requirements to see if they are needed, or only considered traditional from the point of the companies.

The Problem of Race and Gender Identification

Before Civil Rights Laws, companies would ask a person's race and gender on an application form. After 1965 state law forbade a potential employer from asking an applicant his or her race and gender. Further, companies were forbidden to note assumed race or gender in any other document besides the application. Since the whole purpose of civil right laws was to ensure color blindness, who could object?

Of course, the federal government objected. When the feds objected, the very people, who had opposed civil rights laws as an intrusion on the rights of business, howled. "You wanted us to be color blind," they said. "It is only right and just that we all be color blind. We made our records color blind and now you object."

The trouble was that we were now caught in one of those traps where simplistic slogans sounded true. Further, the explanation as to why we needed the records was not as simplistic as the slogan. On most social issues, when the answer is not as simple as the nice-sounding slogans, the explanation is considered to be either gobbledygook or worse yet, *intellectual*. For example, to their way of thinking: you wanted color blind, you got color blind, and now you want Big Brother-type intrusive record keeping that is the opposite of what you asked for.

I actually debated with myself whether to discuss this issue here because I could not think of a way to surface the issue and dispose of it in a few words. I decided anyone who reads this already understands what I'm about to say, or is smart enough to understand that explanations are often longer than the statement of the problem, and aren't necessarily wrong.

Back in the real world, of course, the only ones blinded by the no-race-records policy were government agencies. Ninety-nine percent of the time the interviewer and hiring manager knew the race and gender of the interviewee sitting across the table from them. Ninety-nine percent of the time an employee's direct supervisor knew an employee's race and gender. Ninety-nine percent of the time coworkers knew each other's race and gender. Only the government could not tell race and gender. Of course, name and applications gave quite a few clues.

There was no real issue when the individual complainant was an employee. There were large issues in general reviews of employee treatment or in class cases or in cases in which the complainant was an applicant.

In the vast majority of cases the government (or plaintiff's attorney in any ensuing court case) needed to know, by job title, the race and gender of applicants so that they could be compared with the race and gender of those hired. In group hiring cases, the first thing the government needs to know is: do minorities and women who apply have the same chance as a nonminority or a man of being hired? The government figures this out by comparing the success rate of women and minorities to the success rate of men and nonminorities. Simply put, if twenty-five percent of female applicants for a job are successful while sixty percent of men are, the government wants to know the reason for the difference. If forty to forty-five percent of each gender's applicants get hired, the government does not look further. In the case of the large percentage disparity, the government doesn't accuse anyone of biased hiring practices. Rather, it asks the company to explain the disparity. In the case of the nearly equal hiring percentage, it was not the conclusion that the company hired the best qualified. Rather, the assumption was that whatever the company did was not motivated by gender bias.

After a few years, companies were told they had to ask applicants for self-identification on papers that would be kept separate from applications and personnel files. Applicants could refuse without penalty to self-identify. Companies did not have to identify race and gender for applicants who declined identification, but if the person was hired, the company had to reoffer self-identification. If the new hire declined, the company had to guess as to race and gender.

Companies did not have to be correct all of the time on their own identification for two reasons. First, a person can not be discriminated against for being a minority or a woman if the race or gender is unknown. For example, if my parents were African American, but a person doesn't know that, then he can't discriminate against me because I am African American. (Ironically, I know of a couple, rare cases in which Anglos were discriminated against because the company thought they were African American. Further, in one case, a white man, who was thought to be black, not only was discriminated against, but he, himself, was a racial bigot who objected to the fact that a black investigator was sent in to advocate for his discrimination situation.)

The second reason companies did not have to be right all the time had to do with the fact that we were looking at general tendencies. The African American who, occasionally, was thought to be Anglo doesn't change general treatment patterns.

So, the problem of (perfect) race and gender identification was solved, right? If a person has been in the workforce in the last twenty years, he knows differently.

The internet came along about the time women and minorities were moving in great numbers to professional and managerial jobs. Of course the government moved to scrutinize professional and managerial jobs more so as more women and minorities moved to those jobs. At this point, race and gender identification became more complicated because few people applied in person or on preprinted forms. Companies claimed that the race and gender of the vast majority of applicants were unknown at the time the culling process reached the decision-to-interview stage. At the same time social sensitivity was changing in such a way that more people either declined to self-identify or did not approve of the race choices given. In fact in the last couple years, the government race codes have changed to included multiple race categories. The 2010 census was conducted with these changes.

It is usually in a company's interest to keep the "unknowns" at a high percentage. We would see an application form from a Mary Sue Somebody who went to a local girls-only high school, was in a sorority in college, and joined the female honorary society for their profession, and whose gender was "unknown." A company representative would say, with a straight face, "We can not tell what gender *she* is. She did not self-identify. We can't override that." We would also see applications from a person who attended a local minority-heavy high school, graduated from a predominately minority college (like Morehouse), was a member of a minority fraternity/sorority, and had joined a minority professional group, and whose race was "unknown." I always loved to hear about an applicant named "Lee" that "for all we know he is the great-grandson of Robert E. Lee," when the applicant attended high school and college in Korea and had all Korean references.

This would just be silliness except for the fact that tax dollars were being spent on the investigations, and the investigations were being bogged down and thwarted by the legal hiding of data. We were generally looking at hundreds or thousands of applications per case. As mentioned previously, a few misidentifications did not make any difference in the findings for a case, but a large number did. As Bill, my office partner, said to many employers, "There are boys named Sue, but damned few."

In the last few years, a DOL investigator in Chicago won a case by going to the minority high schools listed on a number of applications for an entry level job for a single employer. She took the yearbooks and matched names and pictures and photocopied them. She was able to show that while most applicants didn't self-identify their race, of those of equal or better qualified than those hired, the vast majority of rejected applicants were minorities graduating from school within a few miles of the company. Granted, this investigative method would not have solved the mystery had the jobs been at the professional level because these applicants would have gone to many different colleges, and the company may not have seen them face to face when they applied.

Title IX Now

Women now make up over fifty percent of law school, business school, and medical school admissions. In 2009, women received fifty-seven percent of all degrees awarded, and this percentage is expected to rise. I even saw a cartoon that graphed the rise of the female degree percentage and predicted the year when the last man will graduate from college in the U.S.

According to *The Economist*, (pages 50-51, 1/2/2010) "The growing cohort of university-educated women is also educated in more marketable subjects. In 1966, 40% of American women who received a B.A. specialized in education in college; 2% specialized in business and management. The figures now were 12% and 50%. Women only continue to lag seriously behind men in a handful of subjects, such as engineering and computer sciences, where they earned about one-fifth of degrees in 2006. By 2011 there will be 2.6 million more women than men studying in American universities."

The lead article in the July/August 2010 issue of *The Atlantic* was entitled "The End of Men—How women are taking control of everything." The article cites Bureau of Labor statistics reports that, "This year (2010) women hold a majority of the nations' jobs—of the 15 job categories projected to grow the most in the next decade in the U.S. all but two are occupied primarily by women." Later it goes on to say, "Women now hold 51.4 percent of managerial and professional jobs—up from 26.1 percent in 1980. About a third of all physicians are now women, as are 45 percent of associates in law firms and both percentages are rising fast."

In spite of these gains the *Cleveland Plain Dealer* on July 25, 2010 led the business section with a two-page article that exposed a $ 65,850 difference in compensation between the genders in law firm equity partners in 2009. The article illuminates well the points I am making, citing polls and statistics over time.

The points they (and by extension, I) want to make are both that the pay gap is a problem, and it used to be much worse. The article mentions that women on the lower end of the $ 65,850 wage gap average $ 499,350 in compensation per year. Americans were more motivated in the 1970s to see women not be denied entry into law school because of gender than we were in 2010 to be motivated to see that women who make half a million dollars a year make $ 565,000 a year.

I'm aware of issues related to the need for two incomes to support a family and the effect of motherhood on a career. This discussion just does not happen to be about those issues. The issue I am talking about is Title IX. I think we've come a long way. To me, the proof of that is that for years Title IX was thought to be about women in athletics only. Athletics is important, but Title IX helped fix so much more than athletics quite a few years ago.

While I support Title IX in athletics, let's face it: The elephant in the room is football.

I love football and have always been a big fan. Despite this, everyone tiptoes around the fact that football is the most expensive sport at the college level. That is, it costs the most money to run and gives the most scholarships so that a team can be fielded. Well under a third of the schools fielding a team make a profit from football. It is unbridled hypocrisy when the cost of the stadium, its operation costs, as well as perhaps operating a football dorm isn't included in the cost of the sport. At the large schools football (and men's basketball) coaches make several times more than the university president. Admittedly, at the mega-football schools, a large percentage of support comes from athletic boosters, rather than the university budget.

At many Division One schools the term, *student athlete*, is a joke when applied to football or basketball players. I understand the argument that revenue and attendance is higher with men's sports because more people prefer to see and otherwise support men's sports over women's sports. I feel the same way on a personal level; however, from an equal opportunity aspect it does remain unfair. In my opinion, college should be less about profit than the education of students.

The realities and absurdities of discussing Title IX, college football, and women's college enrollment really hit home when I was in a fairly recent conversation with a president of a southern state college. The university was moving into Division I, the National Collegiate Athletic Association's (NCAA) large school division. Leadership at that college wanted to add Division I football to the athletic program. To many people, having a football program at the Division I level is a sign of having arrived in the big time (whatever that is). Football requires, by far, the largest number of scholarships of any team in an athletic department. It is also basically a male-only sport. While there have been a few female placekickers, 99.9% of all college football players are male, and there is no sign that this percentage will ever drop significantly.

At the same time the university was moving into the big time in sports, its enrollment demographics were keeping pace with the rest of the country. That is, their enrollment echoed the typical 60/40 female/male percentage.

Enter Title IX with its first standard (but not its only standard) which is to measure compliance as to the parity between scholarships and enrollments. So, if sixty percent of the students are women, with all things being equal, sixty percent of the athletic scholarships should go to women. Yet, football, which is an all-male sport, gets, by far, the largest number of scholarships of any sport. Scholarship trends, women student's wishes, and the like can be looked at for rebuttal to the 60/40 scholarship presumption, but basically the numbers can not be worked out. Starting a Division I football team and yet staying in Title IX compliance was a problem the president of this school had not solved.

If starting with the presumption that a Division I football team is needed at a Division I school, this is a horror story. If one is a diehard Title IX-is-parity fan, it is not a dilemma one cares about. It is the equivalent of imaginary discussions between Tea Party Republicans and Far Left Progressives. They barely share a language, and while certain words are the same, for each of them, the meaning is different; neither is sympathetic to anything the other party says.

In defense of Class Cases

EEOC was the only place where the majority of cases I worked on were about individual treatment. Everywhere else, most of the cases were general reviews of employment or class cases focused on group treatment of women or a minority group in one particular aspect of employment such as promotion or hiring.

A long time ago, the Supreme Court ruled that companies are "persons" for legal purposes. (This is why in a politically tone-deaf manner, Mitt Romney said, "Companies are people, too.") That ruling sets up a real David versus Goliath situation every time a real person goes up against a "person" who has 100,000 employees and unlimited resources.

Government involvement levels the playing field somewhat, making it a Goliath versus Goliath situation. Class cases and general reviews are more efficient than individual cases. Further, in equal employment matters conducted by the federal government outside of EEOC, they go through an administrative law process that is less cumbersome than the federal court system and saves the court system both time and effort. The federal court system is thankful for this and thus grants the administrative process a lot of deference.

Private class cases do the same thing in a slightly different way. The incentive of a large payday allows and motivates lawyers to spend large amounts of money on a single case, thus potentially matching the resources of a company.

Sure, there are abuses. In my opinion, these are mostly in the medical and product liability fields. So, maybe tort reform is needed. The fact that class cases present operational problems doesn't mean that there shouldn't be class cases.

For class cases to be banned, it would be necessary to believe either corporate rule should be untrammeled, or that the government should assume an even larger and more costly protective stance over all issues and go to court as a substitute for the private bar. It strikes me that these are both extreme and wrong positions—one to the right and one to the left.

The Duke vs. Wal-Mart decision concerning certifying (approving) the largest class ever has been handed down by the courts. The decision was against certifying. Many people called this the death of the class case. It isn't. As I write this, several smaller classes of 100,000 members (or more) from the original class of 1,000,000 women are moving forward to challenge Wal-Mart.

At the DOL division of OFCCP, the administration has twice eased the George W. Bush-era statistical disparities needed to trigger deep review of a company's pay records. It would take pages to review this issue for those not in this field, so herein is a discussion of one change that is easily understood, as well as underreported. This change was the lifting of the ban on reviewing classes of less than ten people. This means, for example, that the pay of a group of seven to nine women averaging $ 5,000 less per year at the same job that averages $ 75,000 per year for twenty-five men could be looked at to see if pay discrimination is causing the average salary difference. There are many cases in which minorities and small groups (5 to 9) of women are making significantly less than the men or non-minorities with the same title. This is especially true in the mid to smaller-sized facilities because of the simple fact that the smaller the facility the greater the likelihood that few women or minorities populate a given title also populated with a fair number of whites and/or males. Given that the majority of the reviews are of facilities of less than 1,000 employees, this rule change alone could result in a large number of new cases.

The Challenge of Working in this Field

Over the course of my career, Civil Rights progress advanced, to a large extent, because of the people working for the civil rights agencies. The agitation by outside groups, such as the Women's Equity Action League, NOW, a local NAACP, or Urban League, helped. The discomfort felt by corporate managers at seeing females or minority faces in certain jobs greatly lessened. As I mentioned previously, more women, minorities, and younger people became HR-types. Parents no longer felt that their daughter should avoid a particular graduate program, profession, or sport. Each of these things and more, often at the same time, were the cause and effect of change.

Not all of these steps were forward; many were sidesteps, and a few were backwards. Consider the fact that social science studies around the industrialized world have shown two things regardless of the political system.

First, that any emerging minority group (including women although they are not a minority) will first go into the arts and softer social sciences before going into engineering and the hard sciences. So, it is not surprising that both women and minorities first moved into law and HR in greater numbers than they did into engineering and hard sciences. Are the greater numbers of women and minorities in HR and law a result of hard civil rights work, or just the natural progression occurring in any industrial country? Personally, I think the ideas are interrelated.

Second, consider that these same studies show that after the proportion of women in the field rises, the social status and compensation in the field decreases. The rough tipping point is around forty-five percent. A classic example concerns physicians in Russia prior to World War II. At this time nearly all physicians were male. Most of the doctors were killed in the war, and about half of their replacements were women. At this, the status of physicians fell immediately.

It seems to me that, rather than deny the truth of the study, it would be better to make it outdated. If women make up forty to sixty percent of almost all professions, someday it will be hard for the social status of any given profession to be helped or hurt by female participation rates.

*****

Let me return to what creates federal civil rights investigators who will have positive long term impact. The trouble is that the federal incentive systems are set up in reverse of where they should be. While one seeks promotions, there are financial incentives to work hard and intelligently. However, once the level and city that one seeks is reached, it is true that there is no incentive to work very hard at all. It is extremely difficult to fire a non-probationary federal employee who won't learn or doesn't perform despite being given all the training and counseling in the world. I, as well as others, have fired employees so I don't want to say it is impossible. However, if one is in a supervisory or managerial job that keeps one busy, then it's difficult to come up with the twenty-some additional hours a week for the many months necessary that it can take to remove a federal employee.

Some managers and supervisors get downgraded or fired, which is much easier to do. I have seen it done, most often for the wrong reasons. Generally, though, the higher up one goes in the organization, the more protective the organization is of one.

I have had some great colleagues, but I know of some who reached their level of management by personal friendship, guile, or lack of anyone better to promote. These peoples' offices produced few cases and no quality cases at all. These people often worked fewer than forty hours a week. In contrast, the better managers tended to work well over fifty hours a week without the expectation of additional compensation, and when they worked, they worked more productively. Good managers and lazy, poor managers were paid the same. The better managers had to provide their own incentives to keep doing a good job when they knew they could coast at any time. Of course, this is true across the board whether a person works for the government or in the private sector—it takes internal motivation, and the best employees are always internally motivated.

I used to counsel employees that the greatest predictor of success in regards to promotion was the willingness to move. Most employees don't want to move. Those that do move tend to get a competitive advantage because of the shrunken pool of candidates. Consider the fact that only a low percentage of eligible employees bid on any position in which the candidates can come from anywhere in the country. This means that the persons moving into higher level jobs are not necessarily the best for the job. However, they do come from the limited group of eligible persons who were willing to bid on the job, given the fact that it was located in a city in which the bidder didn't currently reside.

Another problem that seems unavoidable in the EEO investigation field is internal labor relations. We hired people to be suspicious of management and further, to not trust what management said. We asked them to watch out for the mistreatment of women, minorities, and the disabled. Unsurprisingly, the people we hired and trained to be suspicious of management were most suspicious of the management they saw regularly—their own. Historically, EEOC has had, by far, the highest rate of internal EEO complaints in the government.

Finally, throw in the center-of-the-universe mentality, and there are real problems. What do I mean by the center-of-the-universe mentality? It is a corollary to the same mentality that exists at Headquarters. As I mentioned earlier, and will repeat, those who work in the Washington headquarters think they are more learned and committed. In the "field" (anywhere outside of Washington), if there is a preponderance of people in an office who will not or can not move for promotion, who are very suspicious of management, who are particularly sensitive on race and gender issues, and who think their city is in the center of the universe, the manager is in trouble. When orders come down from on high and the orders "on high" come from outside *their city*, the orders will have little value on their own.

EEO Politics at DOL and Politics in General

We weren't supposed to feel political pressure, but we often did. Sometimes national politics figured in. Sometimes it was office politics. My time at DOL spanned the end of the Carter years and ended after the election of the second George Bush.

I retired at the beginning of George W. Bush's administration, but was amused at the shock some people expressed over administration interference with the regulatory process. Had no one lived through the Reagan years?

When the parties change control of the White House, the pendulum swings are not all equally as far right/far left/conservative/liberal on each issue. Administrations are usually far left on some issues and moderate on others, or far right on some issues and moderate on others. At the time, the roiling, jabbering of the political classes is all about how the people they disagree with are to the far right or far left of "the American people" for whom they speak.

In retrospect, and by today's standards, President Nixon and Ford were fairly moderate to liberal on EEO issues. Several enforcement tools used in their era were found to be too liberal or illegal to be used in the Clinton era. "Make up goals" and "Passovers", both mentioned earlier, come to mind. President Carter's and President Clinton's enforcement policies were moderate to liberal for their times, but they weren't more objectively liberal than the policies of the Nixon and Ford eras. President Nixon and President Ford were more conservative, but they governed in more liberal times as far as EEO goes. Even the first George Bush era was moderate, at least compared to the Reagan era. George H.W. Bush's Labor Secretary, Elizabeth Dole, was allowed to be fairly moderate. In fact, Glass Ceiling reviews, in which companies are checked for informal and formal barriers against women and minorities getting top positions, began under Elizabeth Dole.

President Reagan's era was the only era in which the pendulum swung hard in any direction. During his administration, the pendulum swung hard, hard right.

As in President George W. Bush's years in the White House, many people in the Reagan years were appointed to agency head *because of* (not in spite of) the fact that they opposed the mission of the agency. Our agency in the Department of Labor (OFCCP) was not any different. There was no subtlety to the message of the Reagan appointees.

Our first greeting from our first Reagan appointee came at a regional meeting a few days after she assumed her job.

Her first words were: "I'm going to rein in you social activists." In her defense, she was both being consistent with what her bosses told her to do and probably reacting to her less-than-pleasant introduction.

My boss Ray (I've mentioned him before) introduced her by saying that we probably wondered why she was here and speaking. "Well," he said, "They say where does the bear go in the woods? The answer—anywhere he wants." At that, he pointed to our new Director and stepped away from the podium.

Ray also had introduction problems when he was trying to be nice. At a regional management conference, he was trying to introduce an Executive Vice-President of Human Relations. The man had been the Assistant Secretary of Defense for Manpower. Ray introduced him glowingly as "the man responsible for transitioning to the all-volunteer army."

At that, the team leader (and a retired colonel) who was sitting next to me bellowed, "And how'd ya like to have that on your conscience?"

Our new Director and her senior staff were not the only ones just being consistent with the rest of the administration. With the President as coach, Brad Reynolds at Justice was the captain of Team Roll-Back-The-Clock. Clarence Thomas at EEOC reduced the legal enforcement (in Reagan administrative-speak, reined in the social activism) and moved away from the more useful and efficient class cases by proceeding mostly on individual cases. When he had been at The Office for Civil Rights at HEW at the beginning of the Reagan administration, Mr. Thomas (now Justice of the Supreme Court) on July 13, 1981 tried to say that Title IX doesn't include employment discrimination. The Supreme Court held that it did (North Hoover Bd. Of Ed. v. Bell [456 U.S. 512 1982]). He also tried to say that Section 504 (the anti-handicap discrimination law) did not apply to employment. Again, the Supreme Court, that he would later

165

join, held against him in the case, Consolidation Rail Corporation v. Darrone (465 U.S. 624, 632-33 1984).

I first met Director Thomas when he was testifying in a contempt hearing. The Women's Equity Action League asked for this hearing because they felt the government was not complying with a consent order that we had entered into which related to a more vigorous enforcement of civil rights rules. I had already testified about current DOL and former HEW Office for Civil Rights (OCR) actions, and so I could stay in the courtroom when Director Thomas, who was awaiting confirmation as Chairman of EEOC, testified.

I have been unable to get a full transcript of Thomas's testimony from March 11, 1982. The case was WEAL v. Bell at 21 (DC Circuit, 1982) and ended up as WEAL et al v. Cavazos (906 F 2d. 742, D.C. Circuit 1990), but had started in 1974. Without the transcript, I can not quote directly, but Judge Pratt wanted to know how Mr. Thomas was going to shrink the huge EEOC case backlog when the case backlog at the much smaller OCR had risen during his tenure. Mr. Thomas pledged something like good management practices.

I was able to get an excerpt of the proceedings of Mr. Thomas's testimony from that day when he was asked about the timeframes the judge had set for closing cases:

> Q. And you do, down to the 12-month average for compliance reviews you find, do you not, that the timeframes were met with respect to compliance reviews only three percent of the time: is that correct?

> A. (Thomas) That's right.

> Q. Well, whatever numbers you use, it's pretty clear that most of the time you violate the timeframe for compliance reviews.

A. (Thomas) Definitely.

Later, when he was confirmed and running EEOC, we were seated at the speaker's table at lunch at a conference in Cleveland. He was the featured lunch speaker; I was just local color doing twenty minutes of *What's new*. He knew my job included working Affirmative Action cases, and though I never asked, he made a point of telling me he didn't like Affirmative Action. That was his position prior to that lunch, and has been his position ever since.

Hearing anew Thomas's position on Affirmative Action, however, is not why I remember the lunch. Rather, I remember both asking him, "Clarence, would you like the salt and pepper?"

And his response: "Clarence Thomas does not use salt and pepper." It is the only time I ever heard a person refer to himself (or herself) in the third person in normal conversation.

Government Regulations in general

Conservatives need to back off claiming that all business should be unregulated so the market can operate freely. Worker safety, environmental concerns, food safety, etc. were other people's fields, and I'm sure they could argue, what to me, is obvious societal interest in regulation.

Some conservatives understand that EEOC is a societal safety valve for the masses. It lets the steam out of perceived injustice by allowing the government to say it has a (very inefficient) process of one-at-a-time complaints. By contrast, throughout most of my career, we looked at group employment systems at government contractors. Essentially, taxpayers who are women, minorities, disabled, etc. have said: "I don't want my tax dollars going to companies that won't hire me or treat me fairly." I don't see what's wrong with that.

Even the systemic look has been scattered under both Democrats and Republicans. When three facilities of a company are found to have the same discriminatory policy, it should be obvious that an investigation of all the company's facilities across the country be made to check for the likelihood of this being a nationwide problem so that it can be eradicated. Yet, this has rarely been done.

Liberals need to back off assuming that government regulations don't raise costs. They do. Those costs are passed onto us in the prices for the company's products and in taxes to support the regulatory agency. When a foreign government allows its workforce to labor with no protections, it allows companies to produce goods at a lower cost. It can be argued (and I do) that this doesn't mean we should drop our regulations, however, the costs are there.

On a practical level most business people talk about "the government." Including summers and Christmases (at the Post Office), I worked for the federal government under eight administrations. Because of President Kennedy's assassination, I missed the Kennedy administration by a month, and the second Bush administration by two months (my retirement). There is no "the government." There are hundreds of little governments. They are tilted left or right by different White House administrations, but generally operate in a confused and confusing way. Washington sets policy, but generally has little idea of the practical import of its policies.

Usually, measurement is defined by a number of actions of some sort. The dirty secret is that, if the number can't be met, a change in the definition of the action is then done until the number target can be met. Likewise, most agencies carry vacancies. That way, if a small RIF (reduction in force, or in English, a layoff) comes, the agency is able to RIF the vacancies, and no one loses a job.

Regulatory agencies are tasked with producing social good. Often, a significant segment of the population doesn't even agree with the goals of the agency. Social good is more difficult to measure than the production of a given product. For example, take widgets. If a company produces X number of widgets at Y dollars each, and then sells them at Y plus a profit, generally the company stays in business. Social good doesn't lend itself to measurement or administration as easily as widgets.

Shortly after I became a consultant, I was seated at a table with seven various company representatives, who were discussing some new government regulations. The regulations had been issued, and the group raised all sorts of practical issues. Was this or that acceptable? What if we do this; would that cause a problem?

Several people at the table called my (former) office. The administration of the regulations was already in effect for the seven at the table. All had been told that the local Director had no idea of the answer to any of their practical questions. They asked me why the local Director had not given them the answers. They knew the Director was intelligent. What was Washington thinking? Were they trying to spring a trap on the companies?

The company representatives knew companies never rolled out a new product without having supply, staffing, sales and marketing plans. Surely, the government operated the same way?

The simple answer is that the government doesn't operate like a business. None of the five agencies where I worked (whether at the headquarters, a regional office, or a district office, whether as a manager, supervisor, investigator, or management intern) linked policy with practice from the start of a new policy. It didn't matter no matter who was in control.

Civil Rights agencies are staffed by real people with all their limitations, quirks, foibles, and biases. This is not unlike any agency or business.

My personal theory is that the Republican administrations of Reagan and George W. Bush consciously tried to mis-administer agencies whose missions they disagreed with, but politically couldn't kill. I didn't see this with any of the ad-ministrations of Nixon, Ford, or George H.W. Bush, though. Democrats generally appointed true believers with good policy but limited administrative credentials. However, even the true believers played games when it applied to their own contributors. What else can explain the thirty-plus-year-pass that construction unions were given?

*****

In Part I, I laughed at the ironies of poor human resource practices in the human resource subfield of civil rights. Any-thing people do, with their imperfections and mixed agen-das, will be done imperfectly. It even occurred to me that there is an off-chance that a reader may think that my sto-ries are aberrations, that I worked in crazy offices, and that I dealt with the worst of companies and universities. This is not only untrue, but it is far from true. Relative to other units of the agencies for whom I worked, my office unit was always a high quality, high volume producer. Our target companies were dictated by geography or potential receipt of federal money and were no more backward in regards to equal employment as the rest of the country. When I was an investigator at EEOC, I led in the number of cases investi-gated; at HEW and OFCCP, our offices, which had many excellent investigators, often led the Midwest or the whole country in cases and remedies produced.

The key question overall is: Is the goal worthy and gener-ally being achieved in a reasonable way?

I'll analogize food safety regulation with EEO regulation. Nearly everyone agrees food should be safe. A vast majority agrees government action may be necessary at some level and to some degree to ensure food safety. Once the need was agreed upon, then we didn't drop food safety from our concerns because ensuring it caused problems with China or Mexico; because more inspectors cost more than fewer inspectors and add to government power and intrusion; because the Department of Agriculture's dual responsibility to promote and regulate agriculture is a built-in conflict of interest; because the regulations affect the mythos of the American family farm; because food safety affects profits of campaign fund contributors in agribusiness.

All of these are valid issues to worry about. All are details to be worked out. They are not reasons to ignore food safety, though. Equal Employment Opportunity (EEO) works the same way. We have decided EEO is good. Affirmative Action is an EEO tool. Whether Affirmative Action (or any other EEO tool) exists should be debated in the context of the best way to achieve EEO.

Political Correctness

Political correctness is a difficult topic to write about, and that is the very reason it needs to be discussed. It took root sometime in the Reagan era. The agency director from the Carter era was invited to speak at the first managers' meeting that took place in the Clinton era. Ostensibly, he was there to mark the twenty-fifth anniversary of the agency. Actually, the feeling in the room seemed celebratory in the return to "normalcy" after the Democrats had wandered in the electoral desert for the previous twelve years.

The former director ended his remarks with a punch line from the type of joke that may have been heard (and I occasionally heard) in the seventies in a small group of EEO professionals. I forget the actual joke, but I remember the point was less the punch line than it was that among EEO professionals we could make racist jokes because we are in on it and obviously do not buy the racist premise. The punch line had to do with the inadvisability of African Americans and Hispanics having kids because the worst negative stereotypical traits of each would be passed down.

The air left the room before the last words left his mouth. The new Director had to thank the former Director for his remarks and then moved on, but clearly she was flustered as I never saw her flustered again. Sometime between 1980 and 1992, jokes, even between insiders, became *verboten*. Sometime in that era, the N-word replaced the F-word as the word-that-must-not-be-spoken.

Personally, I'm torn on the topic. Certainly, I am not in favor of racial or ethnic slurs, but I'm a little nervous over this type of absolute censorship. It may be all right to effectively ban the N-word, but is it okay to ban *Huckleberry Finn* for its use while missing the larger anti-racial bigotry point of the novel?

It may be that we enforce politically correct speech at the cost of a deeper analysis of what is wrong. Doing this allows what is wrong to stay wrong. Here is an example that is noncontroversial because of its age: women lifting weight on the job. An employer might say (as many did in 1970), "Women can not lift weights and those that try are just trying to hurt their backs to get workers' comp."

The politically correct answers to that are: "Yes, they can; and, you are a sexist pig."

What we did in the late sixties and early seventies was:

1) litigate against state weightlifting laws;

2) tell employers they could have job entry requirements that predicted success on the job (If forty-pound weightlifting was required for a job, a test to see if an applicant could lift forty pounds was allowed.);

3) acknowledge that more men in the general working population than women were likely to pass the test;

4) point out that applicants self-select so that women who have no interest in or ability to lift the forty pounds are unlikely to apply for the job.

On the workers' comp issue, then, as now, we'd probably say, "Are you crazy? Have you ever had a back injury?"

It is even more work to analyze the problem. The response is even more long-winded. The psychic payoff is much less sweet than: "You are a sexist pig." However, the underlying problem is more likely to be solved.

The same thing that I just said could be applied to African American crime rates. Yes, they are proportionately higher than non-minority crime assuming both that white-collar crime is excluded and that drug law violations do not deserve their own category. However, most crime by lower class African Americans is committed against other African Americans. This was brought home to me at a party forty years ago. It was being held at the home of my EEOC supervisor, who lived in an almost all black neighborhood in East Cleveland. She overheard four white coworkers talking about having to drive through a crime-ridden neighborhood to get to her house. They apologized when they saw that she had overheard. She said, "Don't apologize for being against crime. Where do you think those boys go when they get it into their heads to go rob someone? Not to your lily-white suburbs. They come a few blocks over here." Everyone benefits if the underlying causes of crime are worked on. Everyone benefits if crime is reduced.

There are other sensitive issues that need to be addressed, and need to be talked about without raising the specter of being politically incorrect. Moreover, maybe if each side could admit the truth of the others' point of view, the issues could be worked on.

For example, what about the issues of Ebonics/ghetto dialect/hip hop culture? Can any group of people speak/dress anyway they want? Sure, they can. Can American business impose a culture of communication that is required for success on most jobs? Again, sure, they can. I assume if we accept both of these premises and stop bad-mouthing the other side, we can work the problems out.

And so?

In 1967, shortly after he was inaugurated as the first African American mayor of a major U.S. city, Carl Stokes was asked if, when his son grew up, he would be as agitated as Carl was over civil rights. Mr. Stokes replied in the affirmative. The questioner seemed surprised, and followed up. Didn't Mr. Stokes think we'd make progress over the next few decades? Stokes answered that he felt we'd make a lot of progress, but his son's generation would put up with less mistreatment than his generation had, and that they'd loudly be fighting any lingering discrimination.

In 1968, the evening before he was assassinated, Dr. Martin Luther King, Junior, said he'd been to the mountain and looked over. "And I've seen the Promised Land. I may not get there with you. But I want you to know tonight that we as a people will get to the Promised Land." Dr. King spoke those words eighteen months before I even began my government work in civil rights. So, if Dr. King was right, and we were making progress towards the Promised Land forty-some years ago, and it was in sight, have we arrived?

Whichever way I answer will anger the true believers of one side or the other. "Things are terrible," one side says.

"Things are just fine," says the other.

I think we have arrived. We are in the Promised Land, and it is fertile. The trouble is that, left alone, weeds still grow very well in fertile soil.

ACRONYMS and INITIALISMS

AAP-   Affirmative Action Program or Affirmative
            Action Plan

BFOQ-   Bona Fide Occupational Qualification

CO-   Compliance Officer

EEO-   Equal Employment Opportunity or Equal
            Educational Opportunity

EEOC-   Equal Employment Opportunity Commis-
            sion

DOD-   Department of Defense

DOL-   Department of Labor

GSA-   General Services Administration

HEW-   (Department of) Health, Education, and
            Welfare

HR-   Human Resources

IRS-   Internal Revenue Services

OBES-   Ohio Bureau of Employment Services

OCR-   Office for Civil Rights (HEW)

OFCCP-   Office of Federal Contract Compliance Programs (DOL)

OSHA-   Occupational Safety and Health Act

RIF-   Reduction in Force

SAC-   Strategic Air Command

GLOSSARY

Affirmative Action Plan or Program--The pledge or system to audit a contractor's personnel system to uncover any unjustified barriers to women or minorities in hiring, training, advancement, compensation, or retention and the agreement to take outreach steps to overcome any underutilization of women or minorities. In some cases and under different rules veterans and/or the disabled are included.

Availability--For federal contractors, for a given job the number or percentage of qualified women or minorities in through recruiting area

Back Pay--Wages or additional wages a victim would have received but for illegal discrimination in hiring or promotion or because of wrongful termination.

Class--In this context a group of people allegedly discriminated against. If the entity is found guilty, the class becomes known as "victims."

Company-As an object of investigation is called "respondent" by EEOC; "contractor" at DOL's OFCCP; "defendant" in court

Complainant--One who complains; called "charging party" at EEOC

Compliance Officer--OFCCP's term for Auditor or Investigator

Conciliator--The government's term for a negotiator

Double Dipping--Drawing a pension while either still working for pay or while also getting a second or third pension.

The Executive Order – meaning Presidential rule numbered sequentially, abbreviated as E.O.

E.O. 11246—The executive order that requires federal contractors not to discriminate. One of its regulations called "Order 4" mandates Affirmative Action.

E.O. 11375—The executive order that adds "sex" to prohibited basis of discrimination

Equal Employment Opportunity Commission--Created by Title VII of the 1964 Civil Rights Act to enforce the nondiscrimination provision of that landmark law, mostly through complaint investigations and settlement negotiations. It now has go-to-court powers, but Title VII cases that end up in court arise from private litigants.

Joint Apprenticeship Committee--The panel that selects applicants to be trainees
(apprentices) in construction unions

No Cause--Literally no cause to believe the party is guilty; not guilty.

Per diem--Literally "per day". Daily travel allowance

Pre-award--An audit of personnel practices which is done before clearance in order to be able to award a federal contract

Review--In this context a personnel (or educational services) audit to determine compliance with federal equal employment (or education) laws or regulations

Sections 503 or Section 504--Parts of the Vocational Rehabilitation Act of 1973. On the part of federal contractors and grantees it mandates nondiscrimination on the basis of disability

Title IX--The ninth part of the Educational Amendments Act of 1972. It forbids discrimination on the basis of sex on the part of federal grantees. In recent decades it has popularly viewed as banning discrimination just in school athletics. However, all discrimination is banned.

Title VII--The seventh and best known part of the Civil Rights Act of 1964. It bans race, sex, national origin, or religious discrimination on the part of all entities engaged in interstate commerce and is enforceable in federal court. It also creates the Equal Employment Opportunity Commission.

Underutilization--For federal contractors, employing significantly fewer women or minorities in a particular job than would be expected by availability, which is the qualified female or minority presence in the recruiting area for that job. Underutilization causes the need to set a goal to hire minimally at the availability rate.

Acknowledgments

Over the years, I worked with many fine people who are the real heroes in EEO progress. At the beginning of my career, several great people became my mentors in this new field. Later, at the two agencies where I spent the most time, I worked with some dedicated and talented lawyers whose aid with cases proved invaluable, and whose support to me personally is greatly appreciated. Though we always had to work under less than ideal conditions, I found myself surrounded by supportive coworkers and employees who shared a commitment to the cause of equal opportunity. I owe a great debt to them all.

Finally, one of the great constants of my life has been my wife, Jackie. Besides being my partner, she suffered through nightly rants over issues that I could not leave at the office. I owe her more than I can express. It is to her that I dedicate this book.

C.E.D.

About the Author

For more than thirty years, Charles "Chuck" Duffy worked within the federal Equal Education and Employment Opportunity apparatus. During his career, he served five agencies in three cities, Cleveland, Chicago, and Washington D.C. His work also included leadership training and speaking engagements across the country.

Though retired from governmental employment, he still is active as a consultant in the EEO field. His current work allows time for the things he enjoys most: travel, volunteer activities, visits with his daughter and grand-daughters, and hikes with his wife Jackie and friends.

www.ingramcontent.com/pod-product-compliance
Lightning Source LLC
LaVergne TN
LVHW011229080426
835509LV00005B/404